Ready, Set, TEACH!

▶ About the Authors

Billie J. Enz (Ph.D., Elementary Education) is the Associate Director of the Division of Curriculum and Instruction in the College of Education at Arizona State University. She is responsible for establishing professional-development and induction programs with local school districts. Dr. Enz is the author or coauthor of several books on new teacher development and mentor training, including: *The Student Teaching Experience: A Developmental Approach; Coaching the Student Teacher: A Developmental Approach; How to Win the Job You Want;* and *Life Cycle of the Career Teacher.*

Sharon A. Kortman (Ed.D., Curriculum and Instruction) is Lecturer in the College of Education at Arizona State University. She is the Director of the Beginning Educator Support Team (BEST), a partnership between university and school districts providing comprehensive support, training, resources in the areas of teacher induction, and mentoring. She is coauthor and coeditor of *The BEST Beginning Teacher Experience: Program Facilitator Guide; The BEST Mentoring Experience: Program Facilitator Guide;* and accompanying texts for beginning teachers and mentors.

Connie J. Honaker (M.A., English/Education Leadership) is Coordinator for the Beginning Educator Support Team (BEST) teacher-induction and mentoring program at Arizona State University. She is coauthor of *The BEST Beginning Teacher Experience: A Framework for Professional Development* and accompanying facilitator guide; and *The BEST Mentoring Experience: A Framework for Professional Development* and accompanying facilitator guide. Connie has taught at the elementary and secondary levels, and has served as an administrator in various roles. Connie is a recipient of the Arizona Distinguished Administrator of the Year Award.

Ready, Set, TEACH!

A Winning Design for Your First Year

Billie J. Enz

Sharon A. Kortman

Connie J. Honaker

KAPPA DELTA PI

International Honor Society in Education

Indianapolis, Indiana

Printed in the United States of America

03 04 05 06 07 5 4 3 2 1

Direct all inquiries to the Director of Publications,
Kappa Delta Pi, 3707 Woodview Trace, Indianapolis, IN 46268-1158

Director of Publications
Kathie-Jo Arnoff

Editors
Karen L. Allen
Grant E. Mabie

Cover Design
Chuck Jarrell

Interior Design and Layout
Karen L. Klutzke

To order, call Kappa Delta Pi Headquarters (800-284-3167)
or visit KDP on-line (*www.kdp.org*).
Quantity discounts for more than 20 copies
KDP Order Code 534

Library of Congress Cataloging-in-Publication Data
Enz, Billie.
    Ready, set, teach! : a winning design for your first year / Billie J.
Enz, Sharon A. Kortman, Connie J. Honaker, Kappa Delta Pi Interna-
tional Honor Society in Education.
        p. cm.
Includes bibliographical references and index.
    ISBN 0-912099-45-3
    1. First year teachers—Handbooks, manuals, etc. 2. Teacher orienta-
tion—Handbooks, manuals, etc. 3. Teaching—Handbooks, manuals,
etc. I. Kortman, Sharon A., 1964– II. Honaker, Connie J., 1947– III.
Kappa Delta Pi (Honor society) IV. Title.
    LB2844.1.N4E69 2003
    371.1—dc21

                                                        2003-010510
                                                        CIP

▶ Dedication

To the thousands of enthusiastic new teachers who will teach our children and youth.

▶ Acknowledgments

The publisher and authors wish to acknowledge the American Association for Employment in Education (AAEE) and a group of its members for brainstorming about and reviewing this book, and for contributing their knowledge and perspectives of education human resources and career advancement. They include:

- Donna Harner, Duke University (N.C.), President;
- Janice S. Jones, Evanston (Ill.) Township High School District #202, Past President;
- Salvatore Petralia, Lawrence (Mass.) Public Schools, President-Elect;
- Dale Young, Texas Christian University, Board Member;
- Laurie Macintyre, North Shore (Ill.) School District #112, Association Member;
- Victoria Helander-Heiser, Glenbrook (Ill.) High Schools, Association Member; and
- BJ Bryant, AAEE Executive Director.

Contents

Foreword, Michael P. Wolfe *x*

Introduction 1

▶ **Lesson 1** • Establishing Yourself as a Professional **2**

  Lesson 1 Objectives 3
  Assessing Your Professional Style 3
    The Executive Teacher 3
    The Humanist Teacher 5
    The Classicist Teacher 5
  Understanding Your Professional Roles and Responsibilities 5
    Professionalism within the School and District 6
    Professionalism with Colleagues 6
    Professionalism with Parents 6
    Professionalism with Students 6
  Assessing Your Professional Skills and Attributes 7
  Lesson 1 Summary 10

▶ **Lesson 2** • Getting Started before Your Students Arrive **11**

  Lesson 2 Objectives 12
  Becoming Part of Your School Community 12
    Plan Time for Regular Communication 12
    Enjoy the Benefits of Collegiality 12
    Collaborate for Student Success 13
    If You Are New to the Area—Get Oriented 13
  Designing Your Learning Environment 13
    Rule 1: Work with the Space You Are Given 13
    Rule 2: Paper Planning Is Easier Than Moving Furniture 15
  Setting Up Your Classroom: Form and Function 15
    Traffic Flow 15
    Teach-a-bility 15
    Teacher's Work Space 15
  Taking Inventory of Furniture, Equipment, and Materials 15
  Lesson 2 Summary 17

▶ **Lesson 3** • Planning What to Teach **18**

  Lesson 3 Objectives 19
  Creating a Personalized Planning Notebook 19
    Resources for Quick Reference 19
    Student Roster 19
    Attendance Records 20
    Calendar and Deadlines 20
    Weekly/Daily Plans 20
    Long-Term Plan 21

Contact Logs 21
Other Possibilities 21
Lesson Planning 22
Lesson-Plan Format 22
Week-at-a-Glance 23
Lesson 3 Summary 23

▶ **Lesson 4** • Preparing for the First Days of School **24**
Lesson 4 Objectives 25
Greeting and Seating Your Students 25
Using Nametags 25
Using Seating Charts 26
Establishing Relationships 27
Getting to Know Your Students 27
Building Community 29
Learning from the First Day 31
Lesson 4 Summary 34

▶ **Lesson 5** • Communicating with Parents **35**
Lesson 5 Objectives 36
Communicating Proactively 36
Introduction Letter 36
Weekly Newsletter 38
Sharing Student Progress 39
Parent/Teacher Conferences 39
Sample Conference Planner 39
Communicating about Homework 39
Does Homework Improve Academic Achievement? 39
How Much Time Should a Student Spend on Homework? 41
What Is Appropriate Homework? 41
Can Homework Foster Further Learning Opportunities? 41
How Can I Manage Homework? 42
Lesson 5 Summary 42

▶ **Lesson 6** • Managing Your Class **43**
Lesson 6 Objectives 44
Managing the Classroom Proactively 44
Keeping Students Engaged 44
Question-and-Response Techniques 44
Think-Pair-Share 45
Variety: Mixing It Up 45
Establishing Routines 45
Routine Procedures and Tasks 46
Teaching Routine Procedures 47
Correcting Discipline Problems 49
Effective Strategies for Managing Student Behavior 49
Turning around a Pattern of Negative Behavior 50
Reinforcing Positive Behavior 50
Ask the Students! 50
Lesson 6 Summary 51

▶ **Lesson 7** • Measuring Student Learning **52**

    Lesson 7 Objectives 53

    Using Multiple Types of Measurements 53

    Summarizing Student Achievement with Grades 53

        Symbolic Systems 53

        Report Cards 55

        Grade Books 55

        Portfolios 55

    Allowing Student Options with Learning Contracts 57

    Setting Expectations with Assessment Rubrics 58

    Lesson 7 Summary 59

▶ **Lesson 8** • Handling It All **60**

    Lesson 8 Objectives 61

    Managing Stress 61

        Assessing Your Stress Level 61

        Recognizing Symptoms of Stress 61

        Relieving Stress and Gaining Positive Energy 63

    Managing Time 64

        Before School 64

        Noon Break 64

        Student Jobs 64

        After School 64

        Plan for Tomorrow—Today 65

        Prioritize 65

        Confer with Experienced Colleagues 65

    Planning for the Substitute 65

    Lesson 8 Summary 66

▶ **Lesson 9** • Growing Professionally **67**

    Lesson 9 Objectives 68

    Understanding the Life Cycle of the Career Teacher 68

        Novice Phase 68

        Apprentice Phase 68

        Professional Phase 68

        Expert Phase 69

        Distinguished Phase 69

        Emeritus Phase 69

    Transitioning from Novice to Apprentice 70

    Seeking Professional Resources 71

        Print Materials 71

        Web Sites 72

    Lesson 9 Summary 73

    Final Thoughts 74

References 75

Index 76

Foreword

Ready, Set, Teach! A Winning Design for Your First Year appropriately describes the starting place for a new teaching position. Now that your university coursework is completed, your initial state certification is in hand, your student teaching is finished, and you've landed a teaching position or are in process of doing so, you may think that the preparation is over. Actually, you've just reached a new beginning.

Starting your career is like writing a story—a narrative. In Neil Postman's (1995, 5–6) words, it's a story that "tells of origins and envisions a future, a story that constructs ideals, prescribes rules of conduct, provides a source of authority, and, above all, gives a sense of continuity and purpose." Postman underscored the importance of getting a positive start in teaching by carefully creating one's teaching persona and voice. Your journey is just beginning, and it will be exciting.

The first days and weeks of a new teaching position are critical for setting the proper climate for classroom learning and developing habits that enable students to learn, as well as enable you, the teacher, to enjoy your work fully. Most new teachers are uncertain of the expectations of their first job. It takes time, sometimes years, to become an expert practitioner. Experiencing a positive start in your initial teaching position is encouraging and will lead you to continued growth as a professional.

This book immediately will help you anticipate factors important to the success of your new career. Authors Billie Enz, Sharon Kortman, and Connie Honaker have distilled for you the best teaching practices, based on state standards from across the country. Each lesson has been carefully designed to help you successfully make the transition from student to teacher.

You may have concerns about scheduling and organizing your time, functioning within a school, creating a classroom-management system, finding resources, making friends, and setting up living arrangements. You are not alone. Many new teachers experience these concerns.

This book has anticipated many new teacher concerns and will help you make good decisions that support your work, especially within a district-level new-teacher-induction program. However, if you're on your own, use this valuable resource as your personal mentor.

Ready, Set, Teach! A Winning Design for Your First Year promises to help you get a positive start in the important first year of your career. You can do it. Teach!

Michael P. Wolfe
Executive Director
Kappa Delta Pi

Ready, Set, Teach! A Winning Design for Your First Year is brought to you by Kappa Delta Pi as part of the Society's commitment to helping new teachers succeed in the profession.

Kappa Delta Pi, International Honor Society in Education, was founded in 1911 and is dedicated to scholarship and excellence in education. The Society promotes among its intergenerational membership of educators the development and dissemination of worthy educational ideas and practices, enhances the continuous growth and leadership of its diverse membership, fosters inquiry and reflection on significant education issues, and maintains a high degree of fellowship.

Introduction

Congratulations! You are a teacher. Welcome to the beginning of a new school year.

Your first teaching position will be exciting and overwhelming; rewarding and frustrating; energizing and exhausting! These seemingly contradictory feelings are all typical and normal responses. The purpose of this book is to provide essential and highly practical information to help the new teacher prepare and succeed.

Ready, Set, Teach! is divided into nine lessons that take you from planning your first days in the classroom to helping you plan your professional career. The lessons provide explicit blueprints to guide your thinking and practice, including:

- samples and illustrations you can use as guides;
- surveys to help you assess and analyze your philosophy and skills;
- templates for designing your classroom;
- examples of parent communications;
- ideas for assessing student progress;
- suggestions for establishing classroom management; and
- plans for managing your time.

In addition, each lesson includes Mentor Tips for Success, which offer you expert advice from experienced teachers and administrators.

Establishing Yourself as a Professional

Carlos was excited about his new middle school position. Confident in his teaching talents, Carlos was, nevertheless, apprehensive about teacher evaluations. He was unsure about district guidelines and policies. And how would he articulate his beliefs to colleagues and parents? As he sat in new-teacher orientation, these questions kept crossing through his thoughts.

Carlos's anxiety is normal. Nearly all new teachers share these concerns. This lesson can alleviate some of your concern by helping you establish yourself as a professional.

Lesson 1 Objectives

Specifically, this lesson guides you through these essential elements of success:

- Assessing your professional style
- Understanding your professional roles and responsibilities
- Assessing your professional skills and attributes

Assessing Your Professional Style

As a new professional, your views about teaching are still being formed. Yet these beliefs have a profound influence on your everyday classroom practices. Take a moment to complete the *Instructional Beliefs Survey* (adapted from Stamm and Wactler 1997) shown in figure 1.1 on page 4. Then turn back to this page to read more about your beliefs.

How did you do? As you completed the survey, you may have noticed that you awarded more points in one column than the other two. Teacher educators have observed that teachers have distinct philosophical beliefs about teaching. These philosophical beliefs influence how teachers plan lessons, deliver instruction, and assess student progress (Fenstermacher and Soltis 1986; Stamm and Wactler 1997).

Most educators have identified three distinct belief orientations:

- Executive
- Humanist
- Classicist

Though each orientation approaches the art and science of teaching in a remarkably dissimilar way, it is important to remember that all three orientations embody effective, successful practices.

The Executive Teacher

Column A reflects the Executive Teacher, who directs students' learning and focuses on end products that can be consistently measured. District guidelines and grade-level scope and sequence determine what the Executive will teach. An Executive Teacher is efficient in lesson planning, devising materials to meet student needs, and testing on lesson objec-

Mentor's Tip for Success

Your professional legacy is yours to build.

Figure 1.1. **Instructional Beliefs Survey**

Directions: Each box contains descriptive phrases. For each category, find the group of items that is most like you and assign it a score of **3**, then **2** for the next group, and **1** for the least like you. After you score each of the seven categories, add the scores in each column (A, B, and C) to obtain column totals.

COLUMN A	COLUMN B	COLUMN C
Category : I believe classroom environments should be:		
• Task-oriented • Organized, efficient	• Student-oriented • Flexible, spontaneous	• Content-oriented • Goal-directed
Category : I believe lesson plans should:		
• Specify clear objectives • Meet state standards • Meet district guidelines • Be guided by curriculum scope and sequence	• Be composed of long-term outcomes • Reflect thematic units and integrated curriculum studies • Offer students choices	• Extend beyond district guidelines • Focus on depth of knowledge • Include resources (speakers, field trips)
Category : I believe classroom management should use:		
• Positive reinforcement for desired behaviors • Teacher/school developed rules • Consistent consequences	• Class discussion to determine behavior consequences • Cooperatively established rules • Individualized plans	• Teacher-modeled behavior • Student self-management plans • Character building experiences
Category : I believe learning activities should include:		
• Independent seatwork • Direct instruction • Daily or weekly homework assignments	• Dialogue journaling • Cooperative learning • Student-chosen activities and projects	• In-depth research • Guided inquiry • Extensive reading and research projects
Category : I believe student evaluation should include:		
• Mastery testing • Frequent unit tests • Tests that assess stated objectives	• Ongoing assessment • Grades for effort as well as achievement • Self/peer evaluation	• Application of knowledge • Analysis/synthesis of material
Category : I believe students learn through:		
• Logical, sequential instruction • Practicing specific skills • Mastering basic skills	• Hands-on experiences • Group discussion • Developing personal meaning	• Intense content immersion • Teacher transmission • Personal study
Category : I believe the teacher's role is best described as:		
• Manager • Organizer • Planner	• Facilitator • Explorer • Co-learner	• Expert • Mentor • Guide
COLUMN A Total	COLUMN B Total	COLUMN C Total

tives. Students obtain information through sequenced instruction. The content is usually delivered through direct instruction, and frequent tests assess the level of student learning. The classroom environment is highly structured and is organized around accomplishing tasks.

The Humanist Teacher

Column B reflects the Humanist Teacher, a facilitator of learning. This teacher guides students in the process of self-discovery and often uses co-operative learning and self-evaluation. The Humanist Teacher assumes the role of preparing students to learn how to make good choices, both academically and personally. Each student is viewed as an individual with a unique personal history and culture. Student choice is central to this approach—choice of what to learn and how to learn it. To help students acquire knowledge, the Humanist Teacher makes sure that information, resources, and relevant equipment are accessible to students. The classroom environment is rich with books, tapes, objects, animals, and equipment.

The Classicist Teacher

Column C reflects the Classicist Teacher and his or her goal to develop well-rounded citizens through an intense liberal arts curriculum. The Classicist Teacher loves the grade level or subject matter and demonstrates high levels of enthusiasm and scholarship for students to emulate. The Classicist helps the subject come alive through extensive use of field trips, speakers, and experiments. Each student is viewed as a potential scholar, capable of great contributions if inspired to study hard. The classroom environment reflects the teacher's passion for the content. The Classicist focuses on content and arranges for students to engage the subject matter in the way a specialist in the field experiences it.

Once you understand your own professional beliefs, you can articulate your practices better to colleagues, administrators, parents, and students. Equally important is for you to appreciate that professional peers may have effective practices and beliefs different from your own.

Understanding Your Professional Roles and Responsibilities

Though teachers have distinctive beliefs and practices, *all* teachers have common professional roles and responsibilities. Successful teachers are professionals who are dedicated to their careers, seek continual growth, and strive for excellence in their practice. In addition, all teachers have responsibilities to the district and school in which they teach and obligations to the colleagues, students, and parents who compose their school communities.

Notes & Ideas

The following lists detail your professional roles and responsibilities.

Professionalism within the School and District

The teacher:

- Prepares lesson plans in accordance with state and district teaching standards and expectations
- Implements lessons that follow teaching standards and expectations
- Assesses students in accordance with teaching standards and expectations
- Maintains ethics and integrity
- Models appropriate behavior
- Adheres to the required workday hours
- Attends required meetings
- Fulfills required duties
- Completes necessary paperwork
- Volunteers for extracurricular responsibilities and school/ district committees
- Maintains a professional appearance and demeanor
- Maintains a positive and cooperative attitude

Professionalism with Colleagues

The teacher:

- Partners with teachers from other disciplines
- Collaborates with counselors
- Collaborates with special educators, language specialists, and classroom support staff
- Is respectful toward and supportive of colleagues

Professionalism with Parents

The teacher:

- Communicates policies, procedures, and classroom content and activities
- Regularly shares information about student progress
- Documents communication with parents
- Maintains confidentiality
- Actively engages parents in their child's learning

Professionalism with Students

The teacher:

- Reviews school policies and procedures

- Establishes effective classroom management, instruction, and assessment
- Maintains accurate student records
- Maintains appropriate relationships with students
- Models appropriate language use and behavior
- Understands students individually, and develops relationships and plans instruction and assessment based on differentiated learning needs

Assessing Your Professional Skills and Attributes

Successful teachers are self-reflective practitioners. Your teaching skills and attributes are the foundation of your profession, and assessing them can be valuable. Take a few moments to reflect on your teaching, using the checklist presented in figure 1.2 on page 8. The *Instructional Skills Checklist* (adapted from Enz and Carlile 2000) is designed to help new teachers appraise their abilities in three areas: planning instruction, classroom management, and lesson delivery. If you mark any areas as "seldom," you might want to consider ways to improve those skills.

Figure 1.2. **Instructional Skills Checklist**

Directions: Videotape yourself teaching a lesson, and then use this checklist to guide your reflections.

Scale Guide: S = Seldom, **U** = Usually, **A** = Always

S	U	A	Planning Instruction
			Specifies desired learner outcomes for lessons
			Specifies teaching procedures for lessons
			Specifies resources for lessons
			Specifies procedures for assessing student progress
			Plans for student diversity, abilities, and styles
			Plans for all levels of student knowledge/understanding
S	**U**	**A**	**Classroom Management**
			Communicates enthusiasm for student learning
			Demonstrates warmth and friendliness
			Shows sensitivity to needs/feelings of students
			Provides feedback to students about behavior
			Maintains positive classroom behavior
			Manages disruptive behavior
S	**U**	**A**	**Lesson Delivery**
			Begins lesson effectively
			Presents information clearly
			Gives clear directions and explanations
			Uses student responses/questions in teaching
			Maximizes opportunities for all to participate
			Provides students feedback throughout lesson
			Promotes retention and understanding
			Uses effective closure/summarization techniques
			Uses instructional material effectively
			Promotes individual student learning
			Uses teaching methods appropriately/effectively
			Uses instructional time effectively
			Demonstrates knowledge of subject
			Manages conditions for teaching and learning

Successful teachers possess attributes that go beyond skill. Take a few moments to reflect on your professional attributes by using the checklist presented in figure 1.3 on page 9. The *Professional Attributes Self-Assessment Checklist* (adapted from Enz and Carlile 2000) is designed to help teachers appraise their professional attitudes and actions. If you mark any areas as "seldom," you might want to consider ways to strengthen those qualities.

Figure 1.3. **Professional Attributes Self-Assessment Checklist**

Directions: Reflect on each of the attributes listed below.

Scale Guide: S = Seldom, **U** = Usually, **A** = Always

S	U	A	Attribute and Description
			Commitment. I have a genuine concern for students, and I am dedicated to helping them become successful learners.
			Creativity. I seek opportunities to provide unique learning experiences and develop imaginative lessons.
			Flexibility. I respond to unforeseen circumstances in an appropriate manner and modify my actions or plans when necessary.
			Integrity. I maintain high ethical and professional standards and respond to district policies appropriately.
			Organization. I am efficient, successfully manage multiple tasks simultaneously, and establish/maintain effective classroom routines/procedures.
			Perseverance. I give my best effort, strive to complete tasks, and work to improve my teaching skills and management strategies.
			Positive Disposition. I possess pleasant interpersonal skills, and I am patient, resilient, optimistic, and approachable.
			Reliability/Dependability. I take responsibility for my students' academic, emotional, and physical well-being.
			Professional Appearance. I dress in a manner that inspires confidence and public trust; my general appearance is consistent with district standards.
			Oral Expression. I am articulate and communicate concisely; I model fluent and grammatically correct language.
			Written Expression. I communicate clearly and concisely and use grammatically correct language and appropriate mechanics.
			Tact/Judgment. I am diplomatic and courteous when handling difficult situations that arise with parents, students, and colleagues.
			Self-Initiative/Independence. I am an active and creative problem-solver; I analyze my lessons and assess student learning to improve instruction.
			Self-Confidence. I am a thoughtful, independent problem-solver, and I make decisions based on district guidelines and knowledge of my students.
			Collegiality. I take advantage of working with and learning from other professionals by sharing ideas and materials.
			Interaction with Students. I have established a positive rapport with students; I am respectful of students' academic, cultural, and/or developmental differences.
			Response to Feedback. I am open to suggestions and consistently implement new suggestions to improve my performance.
			Ability to Reflect and Improve Performance. I review many instructional options and consider how each idea would impact student learning and class management.

Notes & Ideas

Lesson 1 Summary

In this lesson, you took time to reflect on your style, roles and responsibilities, and skills and attributes as the basis for establishing yourself as a professional. First, you assessed your professional style as Executive, Humanist, or Classicist and learned that all these styles have proven successful. Next, you explored your new professional roles and responsibilities and the ways that your professionalism extends beyond yourself to encompass your interactions with the district, school, colleagues, students, and parents. Finally, you assessed your professional skills as a practitioner and evaluated your personal attributes, with the aim of improving your skills and strengthening your qualities.

In the next lesson, you will explore how you can develop professional relationships and become part of your school community. You will also find some handy tools and practical advice setting up the learning environment and classroom before your students arrive.

Getting Started **before** Your **Students** Arrive

As a young girl, Brenda used to help her dad set up his classroom every year. Now it was her turn! Brenda could hardly wait to get into her first-grade classroom. As she moved 20 boxes of teaching materials into her class, the room suddenly grew smaller. Standing in the middle of the boxes, Brenda was unsure where to begin.

Brenda's situation is quite common. Fortunately, Lesson 2 provides concrete ideas about organizing the classroom environment and a number of suggestions for helping you to become part of an instructional team.

Lesson 2 Objectives

Specifically, this lesson guides you through these essential elements of success:

- Becoming part of your school community
- Designing your learning environment
- Setting up your classroom (for both form and function)
- Taking inventory of furniture, equipment, and materials

Becoming Part of Your School Community

Fitting in and gaining a feeling of acceptance is important to all professionals—especially teachers. Successful teachers become part of the school community by developing positive professional relationships with administrators, staff, and colleagues. However, becoming a part of the school community doesn't happen by chance. Becoming a member of the team takes effort on your part.

The following list provides suggestions to help you form good working relationships with your new colleagues.

Plan time for regular communication.

- Eat lunch with other teachers as often as possible.
- Make an appointment after school to meet with a colleague over coffee.
- Attend all building, grade-level, and departmental meetings.
- Talk to peers who have a common planning time.
- Volunteer for committees at the building and district level.

Enjoy the benefits of collegiality.

- Make financial contributions to community collections. These funds support gifts for wedding or baby shower gifts, hospital flowers, birthday cakes, and cards.
- Be pleasant in the teacher's workroom, but stay focused on your tasks.
- Share ideas when asked, and gratefully accept ideas when they are offered.

! Mentor's Tip for Success

Take the time in the beginning to get organized and think through how you want to manage your classroom. Think about collecting papers, transitioning between subjects or periods, traveling between classes, lunch count, and collecting money. Talk with other teachers to hear their ideas and management tips. Evaluate how their ideas fit into your style or classroom structure.

• Be courteous to everyone in the teachers' lounge. Smile, and only make positive comments *to* and *about* others.

Collaborate for student success.

• Discover who has expertise in unique areas, such as computer technology, art, music, and classroom management.
• Share your talents and skills with colleagues.

If you are new to the area—get oriented.

Teachers who have moved into a totally new community also must become part of the local city. If you are one of these teachers, you have additional considerations, including:

• Housing
• Emergency phone numbers
• Medical facilities
• Child care
• Grocery store, pharmacy, bookstores, shopping malls
• Post office location and zip code
• Utility companies that serve your area
• Recreation, exercise, sports activities, and parks
• Public library
• College or university

Designing Your Learning Environment

The way you create your classroom environment reflects you, your teaching style, and your beliefs about teaching. However, the actual room space you are assigned reflects only the building's age and architect. Classrooms are unique: some rooms are perfectly square, others look like a narrow rectangle; some rooms have natural light, while others are illuminated with fluorescent bulbs. The "design rules" that follow will help you prepare your classroom to be an organized, efficient, attractive place for teaching and learning.

Rule 1: Work with the space you are given.

Begin by drawing a floor plan (to scale) of the classroom you have been assigned. Be sure to identify where the doors and windows are located, and label any unique features, such as a sink, bathroom, or closet. Next, look for electric outlets (you can mark them by placing an "x" on the floor diagram), and then identify where the chalkboard, bulletin boards, and television monitor are stationed (see fig. 2.1 on page 14).

Figure 2.1. **Example of Paper Planning**

Primary Room

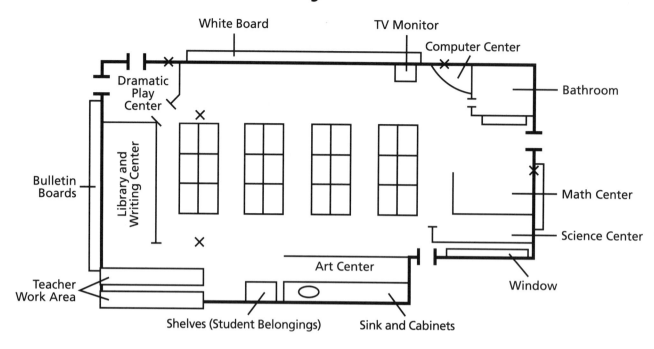

Middle School Room

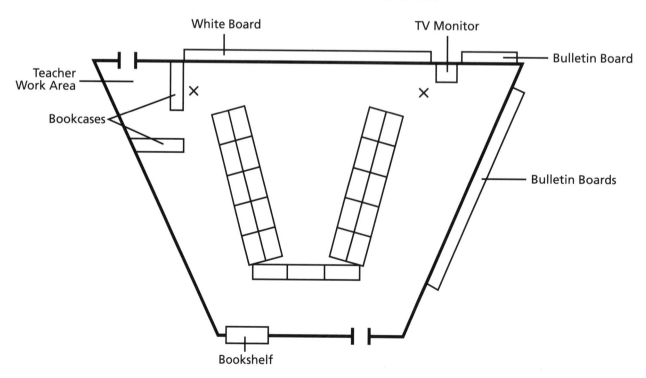

Rule 2: Paper planning is easier than moving furniture.

After you have drawn your classroom to scale and labeled the features, make several copies. Then begin to draw the possible room arrangements (to scale, of course). Figure 2.1 provides an example of how two teachers arranged furniture in two different types of classroom spaces, using the paper-planning techniques.

Setting Up Your Classroom: Form and Function

As you arrange the furniture in the classroom, you will need to consider some very practical concerns, such as those that follow.

Traffic Flow

- Is the access to storage/supplies areas clear?
- Is the path to the exits clear?
- Are the aisles between desks or tables wide enough to walk through easily?
- Are the aisles easily accessible for students who are physically challenged?

Teach-a-bility

- Can all students see the board or TV monitor easily?
- Are students with visual or other challenges seated appropriately?
- Can you view the entire classroom at a glance?
- Does the seating arrangement support your instructional practices?
- Are you able to work with all students in all parts of the room?

Teacher's Work Space

- Are your desk and workspace easily accessible?
- Can you see the entire classroom from your desk?
- Can you use your computer easily at your desk?
- Are all your materials readily available to you at your desk?

Taking Inventory of Furniture, Equipment, and Materials

It never fails that, as a first-year teacher, you will face one of two situations. The first is the empty classroom. The new teacher who has accumulated very little starts the year with no materials or supplies to use. The second is when the beginning teacher inherits the room from a newly retired teacher named Mrs. Neverthrowanythingaway. In either case, new teachers need to begin a thorough inventory of the materials they have or need. A sample inventory list is shown in figure 2.2 below.

Figure 2.2. **Inventory List**

Classroom Furniture

____ Desk and desk chair

____ Tables

____ File cabinet

____ Storage cabinet

____ Computer desk

____ Student desks and chairs

Audiovisual Equipment

____ Overhead projector

____ Tape player/recorder

____ Video player

____ Extension cord

____ Computer and software

____ Earphone set

____ Adaptive devices

____ Plug adapter

Filing Cabinet

____ Hanging folders

____ Manila file folders

____ Index tabs

Storage Cabinet

____ Chalk and erasers

____ White board markers and eraser

____ Paper cutter

____ Bulletin board supplies

Classroom Materials

____ Student texts

____ Teacher's edition

____ Maps

____ Globe

____ Subject equipment

____ Subject materials

Desk Supplies

____ Scissors

____ Stapler, staples, staple remover

____ Clear adhesive tape and masking tape

____ Pens, pencils, markers

____ Paper clips (small and large)

____ Sticky notes, notepads, notepaper

____ Dictionary

____ Ruler

____ Assorted tools—hammer, pliers

____ Glue, glue stick, rubber cement

____ Thank-you notes and cards

____ Postage stamps

____ School forms

    ____ Attendance

    ____ Nurse's referral

    ____ Hall passes

____ Single- and three-hole punch

____ Straight pins and tacks

____ Resealable plastic bags (assorted sizes)

____ Safety pins—all sizes

Lesson 2 Summary

In this lesson, you learned some things you can do to get settled in your new working environment before your students arrive. Specifically, you explored ways to develop positive professional relationships with administrators, staff, and colleagues. You also discovered ways to plan your learning environment on paper and to set up your classroom for both form and function. Making an inventory list of your furniture, equipment, and everyday materials was your last basic task in your preparation for your students' arrival.

Lesson 3 identifies some tools and techniques you can use to help you organize and plan your daily instruction.

Planning What to Teach

As Jason sat down to plan his lessons for Biology I, he remembered his professor's words: "Proper Prior Planning Promotes Performance!" He soon realized, however, that he missed his mentor's expertise and ever-available resources. Though Jason was aware of the national and state science standards, translating this knowledge into weekly, daily, and even minute-by-minute preparation was becoming frustrating.

Lesson 3 gives teachers concrete suggestions for implementing the five P's, including models you can use as starting points to create a personalized planning system and individual lesson plans. Planning initiates success. Begin your plan . . . NOW!

Lesson 3 Objectives

Specifically, this lesson guides you through these essential elements of success:

- Creating a personalized planning notebook
- Lesson planning

Creating a Personalized Planning Notebook

A lesson plan book is key to organizing and managing your time and the curriculum. You can use a standard commercial lesson-plan book or design your own. To create your own, purchase a large three-ring binder, and then organize sections in your planning book for flexibility in adapting to daily teaching needs. Figure 3.1 on page 20 presents an example of a personalized planning notebook.

Resources for Quick Reference

As you plan, consider having the following resources available for quick reference:

- State teaching standards and district teacher expectations
- State student standards
- District curriculum guide
- Schedule of pull-out classes and programs
- "Specials" weekly schedule
- Upcoming school assemblies and programs
- District resource-center materials, check-out procedure, and forms
- Work forms for teacher and student aides

In addition, an effective way to organize school information for quick access is to create an A-to-Z section in a notebook or in the back of your lesson binder. For example, file your committee assignments behind C and the lunch schedule behind L. Label each inclusion in the upper right-hand corner for easy retrieval. You also may want to include other information, as described in the material that follows.

Student Roster

Keep a comprehensive list of student names assigned to your class(es).

> **"I've moved** from what to teach to how to teach."
>
> New Teacher,
> Omaha, Nebraska

Attendance Records

Keeping an accurate attendance log either manually or via computer is essential for tracking and communicating attendance to parents and school administrators. All teachers are required to monitor student attendance.

Calendar and Deadlines

Tracking daily, weekly, monthly, and yearly deadlines is critical. Use a school calendar or your own working calendar. Many schools publish weekly updates for keeping up with committee meetings and paperwork deadlines.

Figure 3.1. **Personalized Planning Notebook**

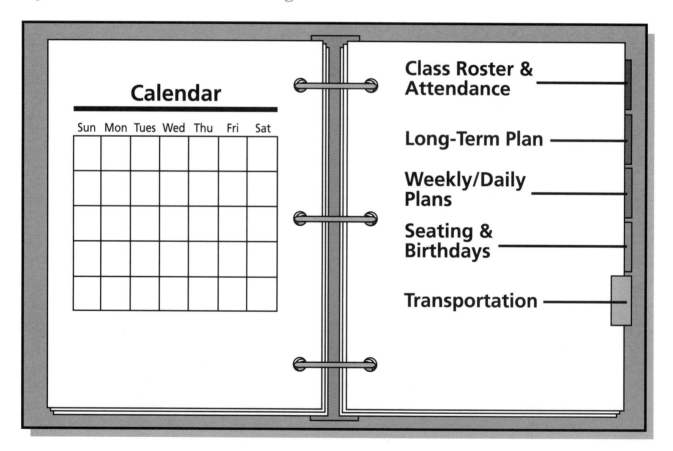

Weekly/Daily Plans

A weeklong outline or overview for instruction and other activities that will occur in the classroom is good to keep handy. This also may include a timeframe with "skeletal" daily plans.

Long-Term Plan

A yearlong curriculum overview maximizes content integration, makes ordering resources and supplemental materials easier, and allows you to make the most effective use of instructional time. To begin developing your overview, review the district's scope and sequence curriculum guide.

Contact Logs

Include students' names, phone numbers, and addresses. Leave space for special notes about the students: for example, parents' surname (if different from the student's) and information about a student's physical needs. Figure 3.2 below presents an example of a contact log.

Other Possibilities

Additional ideas for your planning book include:

- Student roster
- Special class schedules
- School goals
- Seating charts
- Student grades
- Duty schedule
- Special schedules for students
- Substitute plans

Figure 3.2. **Contact Log**

Student Name		Parent/Guardian Name	
Home Phone		E-mail	
Address			
Notes			
Date/Time/Type of Contact	Person Contacted	Communication	Agreement Follow-up

Lesson Planning

Successful new teachers develop lesson plans that guide their instruction delivery.

Lesson-Plan Format

Figure 3.3 below presents a lesson format with questions that should guide your planning.

Figure 3.3. Lesson-Plan Development and Format

Subject:	**Class/Period:**	**Date:**

Objectives
- What do you want students to learn?
- What do you want students to demonstrate?

State Standard: *District Curriculum Goal:*

Introduction
- How will you connect students' prior knowledge to new learning?
- How will you motivate students?

Instructional Input
- What strategies will you use to teach the content?
- How will you sequence the delivery and learning of the content?
- How will students be actively engaged?

Assessment
- How will you determine students' level of understanding?
- How will you document students' learning?
- How will you accommodate students who learn at different speeds and in different ways?

Closure
- How will you help students retain information learned?
- How will you help students apply information learned?

Resources
- What resources/materials/equipment will you use to teach the content?
- What preparations are necessary?

Week-at-a-Glance

Figure 3.4 below offers an example of the weekly plans that can help you transition from long-term planning to daily plans. The week-at-a-glance provides a guide for development of daily detailed lesson plans.

Figure 3.4. **Weekly Plan**

For the Week of:					
	Monday	**Tuesday**	**Wednesday**	**Thursday**	**Friday**
Before School					
A.M. 1st Hour					
2nd Hour					
3rd Hour					
Lunch					
P.M. 4th Hour					
5th Hour					
6th Hour					
After School					

Lesson 3 Summary

In this lesson, you learned what kinds of information to organize and keep in your personalized planning notebook for quick reference. You also explored some tips and techniques for daily, weekly, and long-term lesson planning. In the next lesson, you will discover ways to prepare for and make your first days of school successful.

Preparing for the First Days of school

The first day of school has finally arrived. Shanel has her own classroom, set and ready; students stand anxiously in line at the classroom door. Real faces of students are now matched to names on a student roster list. Shanel is nervous, but excited. She has planned meaningful and varied activities, and she has proactively set up ways to establish a community of learners. Taking a deep breath, she greets her students.

With thoughtful planning, your first day as a teacher can be exciting and successful. This lesson discusses a number of ideas to make the first days of school fun and academically rewarding for you and your students.

Lesson 4 Objectives

Specifically, this lesson guides you through these essential elements of success:

- Greeting and seating your students
- Establishing relationships
- Learning from the first day

Greeting and Seating Your Students

Using Nametags

Primary and *elementary* teachers often decorate their doors with the children's names as a way of helping students find their new room. For instance, Mrs. Bodemann, a first-grade teacher, used her door to "Welcome the Bodemann Bears." She used construction-paper bears with the children's names printed on the bears' tummies as door decorations and a way to distribute nametag necklaces (see fig. 4.1 below).

Figure 4.1. **Bear Nametag**

> **!** **Mentor's Tip for Success**
>
> Always welcome your students at the door with a greeting and a smile! It begins the day on a positive note, and the students know that today is a brand new day.

Notes & Ideas

On the first day of school, when the children came to her classroom, Mrs. Bodemann had each student find his or her laminated bear on the door. Because she had fashioned the bears as necklaces, the children also had their nametags. The design allowed the nametags to be removed easily for use throughout the first week of school. In addition, these novelty nametags helped both teacher and students immediately recognize all the members of their class.

Matching bear nametags on the desks helped each student find his or her desk. This nametag was covered and secured to the desk by clear contact paper to keep the nametag from being peeled off or torn. Using this method, within the first five minutes of the first day of school, Mrs. Bodemann had all her children:

- in the correct room;
- wearing nametags; and
- in their assigned seats.

Using Seating Charts

Middle and *secondary* teachers often need to greet and seat five to seven different sets of students. For example, Mr. Connors teaches three classes of English 1–2 and two classes of English 3–4. To assign seating for the first week or two of school, Mr. Connors initially organizes the students alphabetically and uses the table feature of his computer's word processing program to create a seating chart transparency for each class (see fig. 4.2 below). As he walks into the class, he immediately places the seating chart transparency on the overhead projector. He uses this chart to:

- facilitate attendance taking;
- help call students by name; and
- connect names and faces.

Figure 4.2. **Seating Chart**

Front of the Room—Seating Chart for Period 1				
Row 1	**Row 2**	**Row 3**	**Row 4**	**Row 5**
Adams, Jane	Enwright, Sarah	James, Charlie	Lambson, Don	Roberts, Bob
Berries, Mike	Farmer, Polly	James, Rich	Martinez, Sam	Roderick, Juan
Chavez, Nancy	Foley, Annie	Jenkins, Joe	Martinez, Terri	Thomas, Mark
Delgato, Dana	Honaker, James	Jennison, Chris	Naples, Mary	Warrick, Bill
Dillion, Debbie	Huggins, Hank	Kortman, Kristen	Peterson, Doug	Wendall, Todd

Ms. Martinez teaches physical education at the middle school. She teaches five classes a day, so she has 150 names to learn. Because her classes are in the field most of the day, she finds it important to have her students wear nametag necklaces. She creates the nametags on the computer and gives each student his or her nametag in a clear plastic holder (see fig. 4.3 below). The students pick up their nametags from the storage bag that Ms. Martinez carries out to the field. Any nametags left in the bag are students that Ms. Martinez marks absent. At the end of the hour, Ms. Martinez collects the nametags as the students return to the locker room.

Figure 4.3. **Nametag in Clear Plastic Holder**

Brenda
Bigalow
Martinez • Period 2

Establishing Relationships

Getting to Know Your Students

Though seating charts and nametags will help you connect names and faces, actually getting to know your students takes some extra effort. The most effective teachers want to know about their students':

- interests, talents, and skills;
- home environment; and
- unique learning styles.

Primary and *elementary* teachers often ask parents to share pertinent information about their child. A survey, such as the Student Information Letter shown in figure 4.4 on page 28, could be completed at "Meet the Teacher" night or sent home with the student on the first day of school.

Middle and *secondary* students usually are able to share information about themselves. Figure 4.5 on page 29, the Four-Square Questionnaire, is an example of the type of questions a teacher might ask.

Figure 4.4. **Student Information Letter**

Dear Parents,

I am looking forward to being your child's teacher. Because your child's learning, happiness, and health are so important to me, I am asking you to answer the following questions and return this form to me. I look forward to getting to know both you and your child better.

Child's Name _____ Age _____ Date of Birth _____

Mother's Name _____

Phone: Home _____ Work _____ E-mail _____

Father's Name _____

Phone: Home _____ Work _____ E-mail _____

Child lives with ___ Both parents ___ Mother ___ Father

___ Other (please specify) _____

1. How will your child be transported to and from school?

   ___ Parent or babysitter ___ Bus or childcare van ___ Walk

   ___ Other (please specify) _____

2. Are there health concerns that I should know about? Food allergies? Colds? Ear infections?

3. List any medication your child takes regularly.

4. How many hours of sleep per night does your child usually get?

   ___ 5–6 ___ 7–8 ___ 9–10 ___ Varies depending on family schedule

5. List the names and ages of your other children.

6. What activities does your child enjoy the most? The least?

7. What languages are spoken in the home?

8. What are your child's favorites: TV shows? Movies? Books?

9. Are there other concerns or information that I should know?

Figure 4.5. **Four-Square Questionnaire**

Dear Student,

I'd like to know more about you, from your point of view. Please answer frankly.

Your Name: _____	**Your Family**
List five words describing your personality.	Who are the members of your immediate family? Describe them briefly.
What motivates you? Or makes you happy?	
What upsets you?	What activities do you do with your family?
What are some of your interests/activities?	
Your Friends	**School**
Who are your best friends?	What is your favorite subject?
What do you and your friends like to do?	Most challenging?
	What do you want to learn more about?
	How would you describe your study habits?
	What study skills do you need to develop?

Building Community

A positive classroom community helps students to learn more efficiently and also helps them develop interpersonal skills. To begin to build a sense of community, teachers need to provide opportunities for students to get to know one another.

Notes & Ideas

Primary and *elementary* teachers can use a Getting to Know You chart. Give each child one small sticky note. Then begin to give directions:

> *We are going to make a pet chart. If you have a pet fish, write your name on the sticky note and place it on the chart.*

Use several categories, such as fish, hamsters, cats, dogs, and birds. Another day, you could ask questions about numbers of brothers and sisters, or favorite foods. Figure 4.6 below shows an example of a Getting to Know You Chart.

Figure 4.6. **Getting to Know You Chart**

Fish	Hamster	Cat	Dog	Bird
Julie Ethan Moesha	Carlos Ashley Megan Chuck	Mei Nikki Alex Bryce Nell	Tony Carol TYLER Letisha Allison Ethan	Raul Grant Mei Carlos

Teachers may also turn this activity into a simple math activity, for example:

> 1. *What type of pet do most of our classmates have?*
> 2. *What type of pet do fewest of our classmates have?*
> 3. *How many students in our class have pets?*

Middle and *secondary* teachers may use interactive questionnaires like the Study Buddies, shown in figure 4.7 on page 31. Ask students to complete the questions and then, for each answer, find another student in the class who has given the same response. The other students' names are to be written in the third column. After students complete the questionnaire, the teacher can call on a few students to share their responses and identify their "buddies."

Figure 4.7. **Study Buddies Questionnaire**

Category	My Favorite	Study Buddy
Subject in School		
Car		
Book		
Animal		
Television Show		
Movie		
Actor or Actress		
Song		
Musician		
Sport		
Color		

Establishing a cooperative community takes time, proactive management, and clear, consistent expectations. Parents also play an important role in building community. Lesson 5 provides suggestions to help you successfully establish relationships with parents.

Learning from the First Day

Primary through *high school* teachers need to plan their lessons carefully for the first day of school. First-day planning, like all teaching, involves knowing exactly:

- how much time you have;
- what you must do to teach the concept;
- what you want students to learn and do;
- what materials you need; and
- how you will manage behavior.

Primary and *elementary* teachers should consider the day in 15-minute blocks of time. This tight timeframe encourages you to overplan, which is important because students tend to work quickly while teachers tend to instruct faster on the first day of school. Figure 4.8 on page 32 presents Mrs. Jackson's schedule for her second-grade class for the first two hours on the first day of school. Notice how many behavior routines she teaches and reinforces this first morning. For more information about teaching routine tasks, see Lesson 6.

Figure 4.8. **Mrs. Jackson's Schedule**

Time	Strategy: What I do	Activity: What Students Do	Materials Needed	Management Considerations
8:30	Meat, greet, and seat	Find name tags and assigned seats	Two sets of name tags and extras for new students	Make sure that students find their seats and stay seated
8:45	• Take attendance • Review calendar • Assign helper • Do lunch count	• Respond to names • Respond to lunch call	• Attendance slips • Lunch tally	Teach: • Get-Attention routine • Lunch-Count routine
9:00	Do *Getting to Know You* Chart	Put names on sticky notes and place them on the chart	• Chart • Sticky notes • Pencils	Teach: • Circle routine • Return-to-Seat routine
9:15	Prepare to go to Music	• Review line behavior • Line up		Teach and repeat: • Line-Up routine
9:30	Take students to Music			
10:00	• Pick up students • Return to class	• Line up • Walk in line quietly • Take seats quietly	Star chart	• Review behavior expectations • Reinforce quiet tables with star chart
10:15	Read *Lilly's Purple Plastic Purse*	Listen and respond to questions	Text	• Review Circle routine • Reinforce raising hands
10:30	Discuss story	Respond to questions		• Reinforce raising hands • Reinforce Circle routine
10:45	Create classroom rules based on Lilly's day	Generate positive rules for classroom	• Chart paper • Markers	• Reinforce raising hands • Reinforce listening to others

Secondary teachers typically have instructional periods that last 55 minutes with a 3–5 minute passing period. Therefore, these teachers need to make each minute count! Veteran teachers suggest that you consider the sequence and timeline of activities presented in figure 4.9, First-Day Lesson Plan for Secondary Teachers, below.

Figure 4.9. **First-Day Lesson Plan for Secondary Teachers**

Time	Activity	Materials
8:25	• Meet students at the door • Have them take assigned seats	Seating chart transparency (see fig. 4.2)
8:35	• Take attendance • Ask students to clarify name pronunciation • Send attendance to office	Attendance forms or computer records
8:40	Greet students and introduce yourself	Share some pictures or a PowerPoint presentation of your family, pets, and hobbies
8:45	Review course syllabus	Syllabus
8:55	Discuss school-wide and classroom policies, procedures, and expectations	• Parent letter • Student handbook • Assessment/Grading policy
9:05	Do Study Buddies Questionnaire (a community-building activity)	Study Buddies Questionnaire (see fig. 4.7)
9:15	• Assign the Four-Square Questionnaire (a getting-to-know-your-students activity) as homework • Discuss homework expectations	Four-Square Questionnaire (see fig. 4.5)
9:22	Establish a dismissal routine that emphasizes neatness and orderliness	
9:25	Dismiss students	

Set a large digital clock where you can see it easily, and keep your schedule handy. Most teachers lose time at the beginning and end of the period, so be sure to establish clear and consistent routines that save you time and energy.

Notes & Ideas

Lesson 4 Summary

This lesson focused on how to make your first day of school successful with careful planning. You learned some ways to manage the process of greeting and seating students from the moment they arrive at your door. You also explored ways to start getting to know your students and help them establish relationships with you and with one another. Last, you discovered some ways to plan your instruction time, organize your materials, and begin to establish routines for classroom management.

The next lesson delves into the important topic of communicating with parents.

Communicating with Parents

During his first parent/teacher conference, Cliff was amazed that he and Mrs. Davis could see 13-year-old Frank so differently. While Cliff saw a young man interested in school and friends, Mrs. Davis saw her eldest child as a loud and sloppy boy who was driving her crazy. Fortunately, Cliff was able to help Mrs. Davis appreciate Frank's behavior as normal teen development.

Research has demonstrated how parent involvement makes a positive difference in student achievement and behavior. However, establishing a partnership with parents requires deliberate and consistent actions on your part. This lesson presents a few suggestions to help you start the process.

Lesson 5 Objectives

Specifically, this lesson guides you through these essential elements of success:

- Communicating proactively
- Sharing student progress
- Communicating about homework

Communicating Proactively

Whether you are a primary or secondary teacher, building a positive relationship with the parents of your students is important. Good partnerships are established and maintained through communication.

Introduction Letter

An introduction letter is essential to starting this process. If you are able to obtain an address list of your students a week or two prior to the start of school, you can send parents a "preview of coming attractions" letter. If you are unable to send a letter prior to the start of school, you can send a "first-day communiqué." In either case, it's important for your first newsletter to:

- introduce yourself;
- describe some learning activities;
- encourage parents to contact you if they have questions; and
- ask for parental support.

Regardless of what you write about, the tone of your communiqué should be friendly, and all information should be stated in a positive manner that politely suggests or reminds the reader what to do, instead of what not to do. Contrast these two sentences:

Positive statement: *"Students need to wear safe and appropriate clothes to school."*

Negative statement: *"Students should not wear torn jeans to school."*

Remember, your first written communiqué makes a lasting impression.

! Mentor's Tip for Success

Celebrate each student's growth and accomplishments with his or her parents.

Have a colleague edit your work for grammar, spelling, and, most importantly, for a positive tone.

Figure 5.1 below presents an introduction letter that Mr. Malcolm sent to parents of his middle school students prior to the start of school. Notice how this social studies and language arts teacher also reminded the parents about Meet Your Teacher Night as he told the family a little about his approach to teaching. He also has included a detachable and returnable portion for parents to fill out, sign, and return.

Figure 5.1. Introduction Letter

Malcolm Moments • Volume 1
Anytown Middle School

Curriculum Focus
Welcome back! I am very excited about the upcoming school year. I am Mr. Scott Malcolm, and I am looking forward to being your language arts teacher.

This year, we will study social studies by using literature to understand various aspects of American history. I will keep parents updated about classroom projects through monthly newsletters.

Parents may e-mail me at *malcolm@anytownmiddleschool.org.*

Upcoming Events
Now that you know a little about me, I am looking forward to getting to know each of you at:

"Meet Your Teacher Night"
Wednesday, August 18th
5:00–7:00 P.M.
Room C-17

I will review the curriculum and discuss the rubric grading system I use to help students become self-reliant learners.

Spotlight
More about Mr. Malcolm. One of my favorite passions is reading. I also enjoy golf and swimming.

I also am fascinated by anthropology. This summer, I participated in a "dig" in Virginia. I helped several anthropologists find artifacts at the Jamestown Colony.

Reminders
✎ 1st day of school is Monday, August 23rd.

✎ The school day is from 8:30 A.M.– 2:45 P.M.

Special Notes
PRIZES, PRIZES, PRIZES!

Please complete, detach, and return the bottom portion of this letter. The forms will be placed in a hat, and six slips will be drawn at the end of the evening.

The students whose names are drawn will win ANYTOWN Middle School T-shirts.

I'm looking forward to seeing you!

- -

Parent name _____

E-mail _____

Home phone _____ Work phone _____

Student name _____

Notes & Ideas

Weekly Newsletter

Communication with parents should be frequent and consistent. Most schools now require teachers to send a classroom newsletter on a regular basis. To facilitate this process, experienced teachers suggest developing a consistent format to follow each time you send a newsletter. Mrs. Jones's weekly newsletter (see fig. 5.2 below) uses the same heading each week.

Figure 5.2. **Weekly Newsletter**

Mrs. Jones's
Kinder Class News

What We Learned Last Week

We took a field trip to the hospital. Our trip was exciting, and we learned even more about how doctors and nurses serve our community.

Have your child read you the story he or she wrote and illustrated after our field trip. One of the most exciting stops in the hospital was the baby nursery. All of the children were interested in their own first stay at the hospital. Perhaps you could share your memories about that big event.

Big Thanks!

Our class thanks Mrs. Delgado and Mrs. Ortiz for being chaperones. They also helped our students write their stories.

What We Will Learn This Week

We will discuss fire safety at home and school.
• Our first lesson is called "Stop, Drop, and Roll," teaching us what to do if our clothes catch on fire.
• We will also map a safe fire exit from our classroom and review appropriate behavior during an emergency.
• We will have a school-wide fire drill to practice these skills.

Home Assignment

Because your child's safety is so important, I am asking that you and your child draw a map of your house and design the best fire-escape route. This home activity will reinforce the fire-safety concepts the children are learning in school.

Parent Needed

On Friday, we are going to our local Fire Station. (See attached permission slip.) Because this is a walking field trip, I will need at least four parent volunteers. Let me know whether you can join us.

Special Treat

To help all of us learn more about fire safety, the Fire Marshall will provide the children and their families with a booklet called "Learn Not to Burn." The book is also available in Spanish. If you would like additional copies, let me know.

Please review this informative and entertaining booklet with your child. If you have any personal experiences in the area of fire safety, please let me know, and you can be an expert speaker in our classroom.

Sharing Student Progress

Parent/Teacher Conferences

When parents and teachers share information about the student from their unique perspectives, they can work together for the student's benefit. The best opportunity teachers have for engaging parents in this interaction is during the parent/teacher conference.

Sample Conference Planner

Conferences that feature a positive two-way exchange are the result of careful planning and organization. Figure 5.3 on page 40 is an example of a conference planner to facilitate parent/teacher interactions.

Communicating about Homework

Homework! This once unquestioned practice has conjured up a great deal of controversy recently. While most districts have no policies regarding homework, some districts require certain amounts of homework each evening, and still other schools forbid teachers to assign homework! Many parents have questions about homework. Here are some of the most frequently asked questions.

Does homework improve academic achievement?

- *Primary teachers* often assign homework to help children develop time-management skills and to review class material. According to an analysis of more than 100 studies, the effect of homework on achievement is minimal (Chaika 2000). Moreover, too much homework can be detrimental to family life and student achievement.
- *Middle* and *secondary teachers* often assign homework to further the amount of content the class can cover and to reinforce new skills and knowledge. At this level, there is a correlation between the amount of homework a student completes and subsequent grades and achievement.

Regardless of grade level, research consistently suggests (Chaika 2000; O'Rourke-Ferrara 1998) that the most effective types of homework assignments are those that:

- have a specific purpose;
- have clear instructions;
- have been matched to a student's abilities; and
- have been designed to develop or reinforce a student's knowledge and skills.

Notes & Ideas

Figure 5.3. Conference Planner

Student's Name _____ Parents' Name _____

Conference Date _____ Time _____ Other Teachers _____

Conference Overview
Our conference today will consist of three parts:

- First, I will ask you to review your student's progress, sharing with me areas of strength and areas of concern.

- Second, I'll review the student's work with you and discuss strengths and areas in which we want your student to grow.

- Third, we will review the main points we discussed today and the strategies that will help your student make progress.

1. Parent Input
- What areas of growth have you observed this grading period?

- What are your main concerns?

2. Teacher Input
I would like to share observations about your student's work and review strengths as well as skills that need to be strengthened.

3. Closure
Let's review and focus on what we can do to promote continued success.

How much time should a student spend on homework?

While the amount of time students spend on homework is one measure of the effort students put into learning, research also demonstrates that too much homework may have the opposite effect of making students reluctant learners. While some districts have policies governing the amount of homework students should receive, many districts do not. Therefore, educators suggest that teachers consider the following developmental guidelines:

- **Grades 1–3:** 20 minutes of homework per day
- **Grades 4–6:** 20–40 minutes per day
- **Grades 7–12:** 1/2 hour per class, per day (usually 5–6 classes a day)

What is appropriate homework?

Chaika (2000) also suggests that teachers should assign homework only if it enriches learning or reinforces specific skills students already have mastered. Students should be assigned homework only on concepts about which they have demonstrated a firm grasp, *because students can practice skills incorrectly.*

Traditionally, homework has been characterized as *drill*—for example, practicing dozens of math problems that reinforce the same concept, such as completing division procedures or memorizing multiplication tables. Though this type of homework might help students become faster or more automatic, it doesn't always help them become proficient problem solvers and might cause them to develop a dislike for the subject. *Creative homework,* on the other hand, reinforces the concept being taught in the classroom in interesting ways that connect to the real world. For example:

- To reinforce the concept of graphing, students categorize and count the number of different types of food products in their pantry.
- To reinforce alphabet and word recognition, children find and write down the print they are able to read from packages at home (or actually bring the empty containers to school).
- Students interview parents about local and world events and then write their own opinions as a writing assignment.
- Students analyze television news for possible story bias.
- Students keep a food diary to learn more about nutrition.

Can homework foster further learning opportunities?

Creative homework often is a springboard for further learning, for instance:

- Students who keep a food diary can share this information with peers, and they can categorize and chart their overall nutrition for the week.
- Students who bring in environmental print can create alphabet and word books.
- Students can chart televised news stories for several days to determine whether there is a bias in coverage either by story slant or varying air time.

How can I manage homework?

If the teacher believes that it is important to assign homework, then it is equally important for the teacher to develop an efficient homework collection and assessment system. Many teachers have students grade homework during class and then turn it in to a student who has the job of recording the information (see Lesson 6, Assignment Aide).

Lesson 5 Summary

In this lesson, you learned ways to build a positive relationship with parents by being proactive in your communications using introduction letters and newsletters. Next, you explored how, with careful planning and organization, parent/teacher conferences can be positive two-way exchanges that can benefit the student. Finally, you considered some questions that parents frequently ask about homework and some ways you might respond.

In the next lesson, you will discover some ways to manage your class, keep students engaged, establish routines, and correct discipline problems.

Managing
Your Class

Student behavior scenarios begin to play out in Maria's mind: a student disrupting the class by speaking out of turn; a student dreaming off into space; another student falling out of his chair. Maria wonders how she will maximize student learning when the human element of behavior is added to the classroom dynamic.

Planning, instruction, and management are dynamically intertwined. Proactive strategies must be implemented to prevent discipline problems, while encouraging students to solve problems in socially acceptable ways and manage their own behavior. This lesson identifies successful classroom strategies that communicate respect, responsibility, and accountability for both the teacher and the students.

Lesson 6 Objectives

Specifically, this lesson guides you through these essential elements of success:

- Managing the classroom proactively
- Keeping students engaged
- Establishing routines
- Correcting discipline problems

Managing the Classroom Proactively

The teacher's ultimate goal is for students to learn how to manage their own behavior in a way that enhances everyone's opportunity to learn. In addition, classroom management improves when the classroom teacher:

- is organized and prepared;
- is able to maintain group attention effectively;
- gives clear directions;
- provides meaningful instruction;
- assigns appropriate work;
- uses effective assessment methods; and
- engages students actively in the learning process.

The examples that follow provide specific management strategies for elementary, middle, and secondary classrooms. Use the ideas and forms to establish your own successful system.

Keeping Students Engaged

When students are actively involved, learning is enhanced and classroom management is more effective. The following suggestions provide easy ways to keep students involved.

Question-and-Response Techniques

Question-and-response techniques help students keep their minds engaged and actively involved in the lesson.

- Ask a question first, and then call on a student to answer.
- Give "wait time" to allow students to process their thinking.

! Mentor's Tip for Success

Connect with a different student every day so that you know students' lives inside and outside the classroom.

- Ask follow-up questions, such as "Can you tell me more?" "Give us an example," and "Why?"
- Ask clarifying questions, such as "Can you tell us how you arrived at your answer?"
- Have students develop their own questions.
- Have students give a summary of what has been learned in a lesson.
- Have strategies for every student to participate simultaneously. For instance:
  - Thumbs up/down
  - Yes/no cards
  - Individual dry-erase boards

Think-Pair-Share

The think-pair-share strategy, like its name, has three parts. First, give students something to think about individually. Then, allow them to share their thinking with a neighbor. Last, have a few students share with the whole class.

Variety: Mixing It Up

Using a variety of new approaches and activities motivates and interests students. Some examples of what you might add to the mix include:

- providing variety in individual, partner, and group activities;
- using manipulatives;
- using alternative learning activities, such as plays, presentations, and games; and
- having groups of students teach sections from a chapter or text after researching and designing their presentations.

Establishing Routines

All classrooms have routine procedures and tasks performed on a daily basis. Well-developed routines serve as management tools, save time, and ensure a smoothly functioning classroom. Recommended strategies for success include:

- Identify effective routine procedures that are needed.
- Determine when to teach these routine procedures.
- Analyze each procedure and plan how it will be taught.

Experienced educators and education researchers suggest that the establishment of routines should begin on the first day and continue to be

Notes & Ideas

reinforced through the first two weeks of school or longer (Edwards 1997). Classroom management experts emphasize that using these first weeks to teach routines will give you more actual teaching time during the year, as well as provide you the benefit of having a well-managed, organized classroom (Charles 1992).

Routine Procedures and Tasks

Establishing routine tasks can make classroom life easier and more organized. Figure 6.1 below offers examples of the many routines and procedures that are used in effective, efficient classrooms. A few samples of these routines are described on the following pages.

Figure 6.1. Routine Procedures

Beginning Class

___ Enter/Exiting the Classroom

___ Attendance Procedures

___ Tardy Students

___ Attention Signal

Classroom Management Procedures

___ Rules of Respect

___ Out-of-Room Policies

___ Restroom Procedures

___ Drinking Fountain

___ Fire/Earthquake/Bomb Threat Drills

___ Lining-Up Procedures

Instructional Activities

___ Assignment Calendar

___ Study-Buddy System

___ Distributing Supplies

___ Seeking Teacher's Assistance

___ Storing/Filing Work

___ Finishing Work Early

Grading and Checking Assignments

___ Self-Checked Work

___ Editing Checklist

___ Grading Criteria/Rubrics

___ Recording Grades

Work Expectations and Requirements

___ Heading Papers

___ Name/Number/Class Information

___ Quality of Work

___ Incomplete/Incorrect Work

___ Turning in Completed Work

___ Homework Check-In

Dismissing Class

___ Putting away Supplies and Equipment

___ Cleaning Up

___ Reviewing Homework Assignments

Teaching Routine Procedures

After you identify which routine tasks you need, analyze each routine to decide how to teach it—explicitly. These management procedures must be taught and reinforced until they become routine. Two basic questions are involved in teaching a routine procedure:

1. *What is the rationale of the procedure to be learned?*
2. *What are the logical steps needed to learn the procedure?*

The following are examples of classroom routines that have been broken down by answering the preceding questions.

Attention Signal: Primary Routine

1. *What is the rationale of the procedure to be learned?*

The teacher must be able to attain students' attention.

2. *What are the logical steps needed to learn the procedure?*

Information and Modeling. Give the class examples of reasons the attention signal is needed. Then explain, "When I want your attention, I will raise my hand and count 1, 2, 3, all eyes on me. Everyone should be listening and sitting still for more directions."

Guided Practice. Practice this routine with students until they are able to follow it and you are able to get their attention immediately.

Check for Understanding. Observe the class as students learn the new routine. Reteach if needed. Provide positive reinforcement of the learned procedure.

Notes & Ideas

Assignment Aide: Middle and Secondary Routine

1. What is the goal of the procedure to be learned?

Student assignment aide posts assignments on the class calendar.

2. What are the steps needed to learn the procedure?

Information and Modeling. As instructed by the teacher, the aide records assignment information on the class calendar and reminds students to record this information on their personal agendas.

Guided Practice. The teacher checks as students follow through with the procedure taught.

Check for Understanding. Observe as the assignment aide records the assignments on the class calendar. If there are any misunderstandings, reteach. Positively reinforce the learned procedure.

Correcting Discipline Problems

At times, teachers and students have different ideas about the purpose of class. While teachers are concentrating on teaching and learning, students often are more interested in socializing and having fun. When such differences occur, and proactive measures are not enough, the teacher must respond appropriately, redirect current and future misbehavior, and sustain a positive classroom environment.

Following through with corrective discipline consequences is not as easy as it may seem. The goal is to help students learn to manage their own behavior. The perception of control is vital. Corrective discipline is often punitive and perceived by students as punishments given out by someone else in control. On the other hand, when students believe they are in control, they are much more willing to accept responsibility for their own behavior.

Effective Strategies for Managing Student Behavior

The following list of suggestions provides some effective ways to manage your classroom.

- Set behavior expectations for different types of learning situations. For instance:
  - Direct instruction
  - Group work
  - Independent work
- Clearly communicate rules and consequences; verify/test for understanding.
- Consider the context of the behavior: Is the misbehavior minor or more serious?
- Use nonverbal and verbal interventions, or choose to ignore minor incidents.
- Address the misbehavior with minimal disruption to instruction.
- Use a progressive consequence that aligns to the misbehavior.
- Respect the dignity of the student; separate the student from the misbehavior.
- Follow through consistently; impose consequences calmly and quietly.
- Redirect the student in positive directions.
- Encourage the student to take responsibility for managing behavior.
- Consequences should be reasonable and enforceable.
- Consequences should be reserved for students who earned the discipline and not applied to everyone in the class.

Turning around a Pattern of Negative Behavior

At times, a student will continue to be disruptive or nonproductive no matter what you do to make the lesson interesting and the activity engaging. Sometimes, underlying problems are not school-related. When students exhibit behavior that may be rooted in difficulties at home, it is important for the teacher and parent to communicate frequently. Other times, a student has developed a failure pattern that is difficult to modify or change. In the latter case, the key for changing negative behavior is consistency over time. Do your best to understand this student. Find consistent ways to reinforce positive behavior, and set up consistent procedures to hold this student responsible for negative behavior choices. Your persistence will eventually give you and the student a chance to celebrate positive progress.

Reinforcing Positive Behavior

The following tips are effective for any student:

- **Respect** and value **students.**
- Develop and **teach** clear **expectations.**
- **Provide choices in** learning and **behavior.**
- **Model** positive **behavior.**
- **Reinforce** positive **behavior.**
- Consistently and calmly **follow through with consequences.**

Ask the Students!

Initiate dialogue and let your students talk to you. Students will give you ideas for what they need to maintain positive behavior. Personalized conferences can be the beginning of significant changes in behavior. Use the time together to create a behavior contract with the student.

Putting a responsibility plan into writing initiates important motivation for an expected change in behavior. It provides accountability for misbehavior, identification of replacement behaviors, a plan for appropriate behavior, and an emphasis on reinforcing positive behaviors. It also provides documentation for your records.

Lesson 6 Summary

In this lesson, you learned that the ultimate goal in classroom management is for students to manage their own behavior in a way that enhances the learning environment for everyone. Toward that goal, the teacher must manage proactively, use a variety of techniques to keep students engaged, establish and reinforce routines, and correct discipline problems with effective strategies.

The focus of the next lesson is on measuring student learning.

Measuring
Student Learning

The demands of accountability for national and state standards, district goals, and grade-level objectives swirl in Lynda's mind. Fortunately, from the beginning of school, Lynda had been collecting progress data frequently. This feedback guided her decisions about instruction. Now, approaching the end of the first grading period, Lynda was pleased with how much her students had learned.

This lesson offers practical ways to collect data, measure student progress, and determine what was clear to students and what needs to be re-taught or redefined. Teacher instruction, student learning, and assessment are continuously intertwined activities.

Lesson 7 Objectives

Specifically, this lesson guides you through these essential elements of success:

- Using multiple types of measurements
- Summarizing student achievement with grades
- Allowing student options with learning contracts
- Setting expectations with assessment rubrics

Using Multiple Types of Measurements

This lesson will help new teachers learn the components of an effective measurement system, which includes:

- both on-demand and ongoing assessments to measure student progress;
- multiple sources of feedback for different levels of learning;
- rubrics that guide student learning and self-assessment;
- effective homework ideas that stimulate learning; and
- ways to share information about student progress with parents.

There are multiple types of measurements that assess student understanding. Figure 7.1 on page 54 presents Bloom's Taxonomy (1984) with a list of outcomes that a teacher might choose as assessment measures.

Summarizing Student Achievement with Grades

In most districts, teachers are responsible for summarizing each student's achievement and efforts into one single grade or comment. Therefore, you must consider how you will collect, document, and *synthesize* multiple pieces of information about a student's progress into a single symbol.

Symbolic Systems

The first step to collecting and documenting information about a student's progress is determining what data needs to be collected and how this information will be symbolized (see fig. 7.2 on page 54).

! Mentor's Tip for Success

Understand that not all types of assessment are equally valuable for all students.

Figure 7.1. **Characteristics and Outcomes of Bloom's Taxonomy**

Level	Characteristics	Outcomes
Knowledge	• Recognizes and recalls specific terms, facts, and symbols	• Labels a given diagram • Generates a list • Completes a quiz
Comprehension	• Understands the main idea of material heard, viewed, or read	• Writes a summary report • Orally retells a story
Application	• Applies an abstract idea in a concrete situation • Solves a problem • Relates a problem to prior experiences	• Produces an illustration, diagram, map, or model • Describes an analogy or solves problems • Teaches others
Analysis	• Examines a concept and determines its major components • Sees connections (cause-effect, similarities-differences)	• Designs a graph, survey, chart, or diagram • Produces a report showing cause-effect
Synthesis	• Puts together elements in new and original ways	• Creates artwork, song, poem, dance, music, play, speech, video, or film • Plans an invention using computer programs
Evaluation	• Makes informed judgments about the value of ideas or materials	• Debates or discusses • Writes a letter to the editor • Assigns ranks

Figure 7.2. **Examples of Symbolic Systems**

Effort		Achievement		Grade Level	
Progress	*Symbol*	*Progress*	*Symbol*	*Progress*	*Symbol*
Outstanding	O	Excellent	A or 1	Above	A
Satisfactory	S	Above Average	B or 2		
Inconsistent	I	Average	C or 3	At Level	G
Needs Improvement	N	Below Average	D or 4		
Unsatisfactory	U	Failing	F or 5	Below	B

Report Cards

Report cards highlight information that the district expects the teacher to assess. Figure 7.3 below presents a primary report card for the area of reading. Notice that the teacher will need to collect and document information about each child's oral reading fluency, comprehension, and vocabulary. Likewise, the teacher will need to determine each child's independent reading level. In addition to academic achievement, the teacher will need to determine a way to assess each child's effort.

Figure 7.3. **The Reading Section of a Primary Report Card**

Reading	Period 1	Period 2	Period 3	Period 4
Effort				
Achievement				
Grade-Level Work				
Oral Reading Fluency				
Comprehension				
Vocabulary				
Independent Reading Level				

You must begin to assess and document student progress from the first week of school. The following section describes how to set up a grade book and provides a brief overview of a portfolio evaluation system.

Grade Books

Grade books, or computer programs that record grades, document the numeric or alpha symbols that summarize student achievement. Notice how the grade book shown in figure 7.4 on page 56 has been organized to reflect the categories on the report card in the order they appear on the report card (refer to fig. 7.3). Symbols alone, however, do not provide enough information to document a student's progress and explain why particular grades were earned. Therefore, teachers should use portfolios to share that information.

Portfolios

Portfolios contain weekly assignments, unit tests, district criterion-referenced tests, and other information, such as anecdotal notes, or audio

Figure 7.4. **Examples of Grade Book Entries**

	Level	Period 1			Period 2			Period 3			Period 4			Reported Grades			
		Fluency	Comprehension	Effort	Fluency	Comprehension	Effort	Fluency	Comprehension	Effort	Fluency	Comprehension	Effort	Level	Fluency	Comprehension	Effort
Carmen	B	1	1	S	1	1	S	1	1	S	1	1	S	B	1	1	S
Joseph	G	3	1	N	3	1	N	3	1	N	2+	1	N	G	3	1	N

or videotapes of student performance. This information can be organized in the portfolio and easily accessed when the reporting period ends. The portfolio allows the teacher an opportunity to share samples of a student's work with parents. Further, it allows the teacher, student, and parents to see progress over time.

To create a portfolio, you may use a sturdy two-pocket folder with center tabs that help to organize observational notes in a sequential manner. A zippered pouch may be used to hold video- or audiotapes. Figure 7.5 below shows an example of an elementary portfolio.

Figure 7.5. **Elementary Portfolio with Inserts for Anecdotal Notes**

Allowing Student Options with Learning Contracts

No single evaluation strategy works well for all subjects, grade levels, or student learning styles. To illustrate this point, consider Ms. Turner, a middle school math/science teacher, who has implemented an approach that allows students multiple ways to demonstrate and document their understanding of the content they are learning. Ms. Turner uses learning contracts and assessment rubrics.

A learning contract allows students options for demonstrating their growing understanding. Figure 7.6 below offers an example of a learning contract.

Figure 7.6. Example of a Learning Contract

I, _____ , a student in Ms. Turner's math-science class, do hereby contract to complete the following learning goals during my investigation of Sea Mammals. I agree to complete these tasks by _____. I understand that I am agreeing to earn a(n) ____. Therefore I know I will need to earn between ____ and ____ points. I understand that the point values listed below are the maximum number that can be earned for each task and that fewer points may be awarded.

- I also understand that certain assignments are required = **R.**
- I have identified my other choices with an **X.**
- Items marked with an * have rubrics that will help me develop the project.

Points Needed to Earn Specific Grades

> 90 = A	> 80 = B	> 70 = C	> 60 = D	> 50 = F

R	/05 pts	Read Chapter 4 in the text; do exercises on page 60.
R	/05 pts	Matching quiz
R	/05 pts	True/False quiz
R	/05 pts	Multiple-Choice quiz
R	/05 pts	Short-Answer quiz
	/20 pts	Diagram—labeling a sea mammal*
	/20 pts	Model of a sea mammal*
	/20 pts	Presentation on a sea mammal's habitat and life*
	/20 pts	Literature review—research summary*
	/20 pts	Special student-designed, teacher-approved project
R	/30 pts	Sea mammal booklet*
R	/05 pts	Student/teacher assessment of effort*

Total Points	Grade Earned

Student signature	Teacher signature	Parent signature	Date

Setting Expectations with Assessment Rubrics

Aside from learning contracts, Ms. Turner also uses assessment rubrics, which are designed to help students understand the expectations for their assignments (see figs. 7.7, 7.8, and 7.9 that follow).

Figure 7.7. Rubric for Research Project for the Sea Mammals Unit

Student:		Teacher:
Subject:	Period:	Date:

This is a record of research skills demonstrated by this student. The student initials **(SI)** and the teacher's score **(TS)** indicate that the skill was successfully demonstrated. It is each student's task to bring this form and the documentation to the teacher for review.

SI	TS	Research Skill
		Located a book on sea mammals. Cite book:
		Used Internet to find three research articles on sea mammals.
		Summarized (one page) each research article. Cite articles and attach summaries.
	/05	1.
	/05	2.
	/05	3.
	/05	Written summary (2 paragraphs) interpreting graph, chart, or diagram. Attach summary with graph, chart, or diagram.
Total	**/20**	Comments:

Figure 7.8. Diagram—Model Scoring Rubric

Student:		Teacher:
Subject:	Period:	Date:

The student and teacher will evaluate the diagram or model.

The student assigns: **O** = Outstanding   **S** = Satisfactory   **N** = Needs Improvement.

The teacher assigns a score of **0–4** for a total possible score of 20.

Student Rating	Focus of Assessment	Teacher's Score
	Elements of the model or diagram are accurate in shape.	/04
	Elements of the model or diagram are accurate in scale.	/04
	Labeling is accurate and legible.	/04
	Legend is accurate and legible.	/04
	Model or diagram is visually interesting and pleasing.	/04
Comments:		**/20 Total**

Figure 7.9. **Student and Teacher Assessment of Effort**

Student:	Subject:	Date:

Directions: The student completes the Student Evaluation column and the lower section of this evaluation, and then the teacher completes the Teacher Evaluation column. Afterward, student and teacher discuss the accomplishments of the student, decide on areas that need to be improved, and plan goals for future learning experiences.

Student Evaluation = **SE**   Teacher Evaluation = **TE**

O = Outstanding   **S** = Satisfactory   **I** = Inconsistent   **N** = Needs Improvement

SE	TE	Assessment Statement
		I completed all readings and assignments for this unit on time.
		I showed growth in my planning and organizational skills.
		I have gained skills in doing research.
		I have gained skills in taking notes to gather information.
		I used a variety of relevant resources to learn about my subject.
		I am able to evaluate my own accomplishments fairly.
		I identified what I need to improve accurately and honestly.

The most important thing I learned in this unit was:

Regarding my work in this unit, I am most proud of:

New learning goals:

Lesson 7 Summary

In this lesson, you learned some techniques for collecting data and measuring student progress. You were introduced to various types of measurements and grading systems, as well as learning contracts and assessment rubrics.

The next lesson focuses on handling some of the challenges that go along with teaching, including managing stress, managing time, and planning for a substitute.

Handling It All

Creating lesson plans, tracking attendance, preparing substitute teacher materials, grading papers . . . a teacher's workload continues well beyond the hours spent teaching. This reality sets in for Steve as the beginning weeks of school turn into months. Unfortunately, the teaching certificate did not magically give him more time in the day. It has taken some effort and time-management skills, but Steve now has developed a system that allows him to walk away from his classroom with a sense of accomplishment for that day. He gives himself permission to make the transition to devoting time and energy to balance himself professionally and personally.

This lesson offers practical advice on managing time and dealing with stresses associated with the profession. Also included are tips for preparing for a substitute teacher.

Lesson 8 Objectives

Specifically, this lesson guides you through these essential elements of success:

- Managing stress
- Managing time
- Planning for the substitute

Managing Stress

Before you can get a handle on managing stress, you need to assess your stress level and learn to recognize your own stress signals. Once you know your personal patterns, you can employ some techniques for alleviating the stress and gaining personal energy.

Assessing Your Stress Level

Stress is a product of many variables interacting with one another. The survey in figure 8.1 on page 62 allows you to pre-assess factors that may contribute to your stress level. Complete the survey, and then return to this text.

Analyze your responses on the survey. Though you cannot turn back time, or change your preparation or the culture of your current school environment, you can use the suggestions here to manage some variables that generate stress.

Recognizing Symptoms of Stress

New faces, new responsibilities, new surroundings—these factors often will cause a sense of being "stressed." However, too much stress can cause physical problems. If you are experiencing any of these symptoms, or a combination of these symptoms, it is important that you seek a doctor's attention. Mental and physical stress symptoms are your body's way of telling you to take it easy and put balance into your life. Symptoms frequently associated with severe stress include:

- recurring headaches;
- laryngitis;
- stomach problems;
- frequent heartburn;

! Mentor's Tip for Success

Give yourself permission to be human and to have a life outside of school.

Figure 8.1. **Assessing-Your-Stress Survey**

Directions: For each category, choose between the statements in columns X and Y to determine which one is the most true for you, and put a check next to that statement.

POTENTIAL STRESSORS	COLUMN X	COLUMN Y
Teacher Preparation	☐ My teacher education program did a very good job in preparing me.	☐ My teacher education program did a fair job in preparing me.
Prior Experiences	☐ I've had many experiences working with students (500–1,000 hours)	☐ I've had some experiences working with students (less than 500 hours)
Preparation Match	☐ My student teaching experience (grade level or subject matter) was an exact match to my current job.	☐ My student teaching experience (grade level or subject matter) was different from my current job.
Culture Match	☐ The students I worked with in student teaching were similar to the students in my current job (SES, language, culture).	☐ The students I worked with in student teaching were different from the students in my current job (SES, language, culture).
Health	☐ I am in good health and have a high energy level.	☐ I am in fair health and have an average energy level.
Personal Life	☐ I have a secure and stable home life.	☐ I have changes or challenges in my home life.
Commitments	☐ I have some family responsibilities.	☐ I have quite a few family responsibilities.
Organizational Skills	☐ I am organized. I *like* to handle multiple tasks.	☐ I am somewhat organized. I can handle multiple tasks.
Interpersonal Skills	☐ I enjoy working with adults and students. I am always pleasant.	☐ I can work with adults and students. I am usually pleasant.
Dealing with Change	☐ I am flexible. Change is a welcome challenge.	☐ I can manage change, but I prefer knowing what to expect.
	☐ COLUMN X Total	☐ COLUMN Y Total

Scoring Guide: For every answer you marked in column X, give yourself 1 point. For every answer you marked in column Y, give yourself 2 points. Total each column. **If you scored 10:** Congratulations! You have few potential stressors. **If you scored 11–17:** Good. You have an average number of stressors. **If you scored 18–20:** Take it easy! You have a number of stressors. Be sure to seek support.

- hostile feelings and language;
- depression and crying;
- sudden weight changes;
- tense back and neck muscles; and
- unrelenting exhaustion.

Relieving Stress and Gaining Positive Energy

Use the following stress relievers to gain positive energy:

- Stand up and do stretching exercises.
- List five things you have enjoyed in the last month.
- List five things you would like to do in the next month.
- Think of some funny event from your life. Laugh out loud.
- Put on some upbeat music and dance.

Managing Time

Successful teachers have developed dozens of strategies for making the most of the hidden minutes and seconds that are scattered throughout the day. These teachers have developed timesaving procedures and have taught their students how to help with activities such as filing, alphabetizing, and grading. The following suggestions will help you manage time and stress.

Before School

Eat breakfast. Arrive at least a half hour early. Review your plans and materials one more time before class starts.

Noon Break

Eat lunch. Socialize for a few minutes. Laughing or commiserating with your colleagues is important; it helps keep you energized.

Student Jobs

Ask students to clean around their desks and return materials to their proper places at the end of each period or at the end of each day.

After School

Have a snack. Establish an after-school routine. Save time by knowing what needs to be done, and then do it. For instance:

- **Review calendar.** Use one monthly calendar. Record both school and personal activities immediately, and update regularly. Determine what needs to be accomplished, and confirm appointments.

- **Sort mail.** Read through mail at the end of the day. Throw away junk mail. Record important dates and deadlines on your calendar immediately, and then throw away the actual notice, if possible. File important documents, and answer requests immediately.
- **Respond to e-mail and phone messages.** Set aside time at the end of each day to return phone messages and e-mails. Be sure to document phone calls and save important e-mail communications.

Plan for Tomorrow—Today

Prepare for tomorrow's lessons tonight. Ready all the instructional materials, lesson plans, assessments, and other related items.

Prioritize

Separate important tasks from less critical ones. What is essential to your success tomorrow? Can you delegate less important tasks to a student helper, classroom aide, or parent volunteer?

Confer with Experienced Colleagues

Working with experienced colleagues helps to lighten the load. Often, they can offer lessons, help you find resources and materials, and also lend compassionate support. Their wisdom and humor will help you work through the challenging days and rejoice in the inspirational moments.

Planning for the Substitute

Even if you "have not had a cold in years," the likelihood of teachers needing the services of a substitute teacher is high. At the end of each day, prepare for the possibility of a substitute the following day. Collect and organize teaching materials, and place the "sub" folder on top. That way you are always ready for tomorrow, no matter what happens.

A simple way to organize a substitute folder is to label a folder or a three-ring binder to hold lists and memos pertinent to your daily routine (see fig. 8.2 on page 66). Inside the folder, you may wish to include the following items:

1. Seating chart(s)
2. School schedule
3. Outline of your daily schedule
4. List of ability and interest groups
5. Names of students, by class period, who are helpful

Notes & Ideas

6. Names of students, by class period, who need special attention
7. Names of helpful teachers, including aide and resource teachers
8. List of parent volunteers (names, days, times)
9. List of how students are transported (special services)

Figure 8.2. **Substitute Folder**

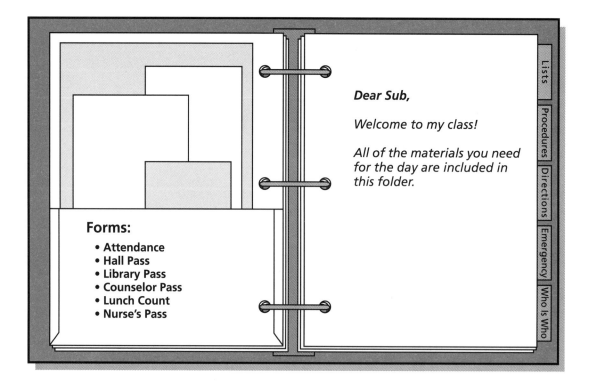

Lesson 8 Summary

In this lesson, you took time to assess your own stress level, to review common symptoms of stress, and to consider various techniques you might use to relieve your stress and regain your energy. Next, you explored some important time-management strategies. And, finally, you reviewed a simple system for organizing materials for a substitute.

The next, and final, lesson of this book gives you some guidance for planning your professional growth and teaching career.

Growing Professionally

Finishing a long day, veteran Darla was tired and just wanted to go home. Sophomores and algebra don't always mix well, she thought. Just then, a knock at the door reminded Darla that she had promised her new colleague, Kara, that they could review the next unit together. For a moment, Darla considered canceling their meeting, but Kara's eager face changed her mind. A few minutes later, Kara and Darla were sharing laughs, ideas, and plans.

In the quest for lifelong learning and career satisfaction, understanding the life cycle of the career teacher is essential. That understanding will provide the focus for growth with motivation and inspiration. Begin your pursuit of emeritus.

Understanding the Life Cycle of the Career Teacher

Teaching is a highly complex profession. Teachers, like doctors and lawyers, improve with practice over time. The *Life Cycle of the Career Teacher* model (Steffy, Wolfe, Pasch, and Enz 2000) is based on the premise that, given the appropriate learning environment, all teachers will continue to grow and develop throughout their professional lifetime. The model identifies six phases of teacher development: Novice, Apprentice, Professional, Expert, Distinguished, and Emeritus.

Novice Phase

The *Novice phase* begins when preservice students first encounter practicum experiences as part of their teacher education program. This phase continues through student teaching.

Apprentice Phase

The *Apprentice phase* begins when teachers receive responsibility for planning and delivering instruction on their own. This phase continues until integration and synthesis of knowledge, pedagogy, and confidence emerges. Typically, the apprentice phase includes the induction period and extends into the second or third year of teaching.

Professional Phase

The *Professional phase* emerges as teachers grow in their self-confidence as educators. Student feedback plays a critical role in this process. Students' respect for teachers and teachers' respect for students form the bedrock foundation on which this stage is built.

"The deeper we search, the more we find there is to know and, as long as human life exists, I believe that it will always be so."

Albert Einstein,
Kappa Delta Pi Laureate

Expert Phase

The *Expert phase* symbolizes achievement of the highest standards. Even if they do not seek it formally, these teachers meet the expectations required for national board certification.

Distinguished Phase

The *Distinguished phase* is reserved for teachers who are truly gifted—the "pied pipers" of the profession. Distinguished teachers impact education-related decisions at city, state, and national levels.

Emeritus Phase

The *Emeritus phase* marks a lifetime of achievement in education. Teachers who retire after a lifetime of teaching deserve society's recognition and praise. Often, they continue to serve the profession as tutors or mentors.

Teachers' skills and knowledge grow through a process of continuous reflection in the reflection-renewal-growth cycle. Figure 9.1 below offers a graphic representation of the cycle.

Notes & Ideas

Figure 9.1. **Reflection-Renewal-Growth Cycle Model**

Transitioning from Novice to Apprentice

You will progress from one phase to another as you determine how to deal with the major concerns you are faced with at each phase along the continuum of teacher development. Following are the major concerns and suggestions for growth at the Novice and Apprentice phases.

Concern: How do I make the transition from student to teacher, school to work?
Suggestion: Making this transition will be smoothest if you follow the lead of teacher educators who are modeling reflective practices and guiding you through this process. Look to teacher educators, for example, to:

- connect prior experiences and beliefs to new knowledge;
- offer explicit examples of how theory is translated to practice; and
- provide instruction and practice in reflective processes.

Concern: The reality of classroom life is overwhelming. How do I cope?
Suggestion: Again, teacher educators/mentors can provide you with explicit instruction and model the basics of managing a classroom. They can help you, for instance, to:

- organize instructional content;
- implement and maintain classroom routines; and
- assess and share student performance—e.g., report cards and portfolios.

Concern: How can I develop instructional skills and behavior-management strategies?
Suggestion: With the help of teacher educators/mentors, you can learn classroom-observation techniques. This will help you to:

- build your professional vocabulary and assess your own instructional performance;
- determine cause and effect, teacher actions, and student behavior; and
- evaluate other teachers' instructional planning and delivery.

Concern: I am overwhelmed by full-time responsibilities. What do I do?
Suggestion: Participate in developmentally sequenced workshops that are:

- timely and offer sufficient information;
- explicit and include models and specific examples; and
- accommodate individual needs.

Concern: How can I achieve competence and acceptance within my school district?

Suggestion: Work closely with a prepared mentor who can offer you context-specific information and who can:

- review district curriculum with you and offer successful methods;
- identify and locate appropriate instructional resources and materials; and
- respond to your emerging needs on a daily basis.

Concern: I'm not sure that I made the right career choice. What now?

Suggestion: Join an apprentice-teacher cohort group that can provide you with psychological support by:

- discussing common concerns and needs;
- problem-solving and determining appropriate solutions;
- building community within the school and across the district; and
- sharing ideas, materials, and strategies.

Concern: My school or district disregards apprentice teachers. How can I get the support I need?

Suggestion: Work with other teachers and your school administration to help develop new teacher–friendly schools. Share your concerns and encourage your school system to provide:

- an optimum teaching load;
- realistic class/student assignments;
- comprehensive induction programs; and
- time to confer/observe other teachers.

Seeking Professional Resources

Educators today are fortunate to have so many resources available to them. Professional journals, Web sites, conferences, books, and other sources offer you, a developing professional, many options for learning and growing. Following are just a few recommended resources.

Print Materials

Edwards, C. H. 1997. *Classroom discipline & management.* Columbus, Ohio: Merrill.

Enz, B., C. Honaker, and S. Kortman. 2002. *Trade secrets: Tips, tools, and timesavers for middle and secondary teachers.* Dubuque, Iowa: Kendall-Hunt.

Notes & Ideas

Enz, B., S. Kortman, and C. Honaker. 2002. *Trade secrets: Tips, tools, and timesavers for primary and elementary teachers*. Dubuque, Iowa: Kendall-Hunt.

Hammeken, P. A. 1995. *450 strategies for success: A practical guide for all educators who teach students with disabilities*. Minnetonka, Minn.: Peytral.

Jones, V. F., and L. S. Jones. 1995. *Comprehensive classroom management: Creating positive learning environments for all students*, 4th ed. Needham Heights, Mass: Allyn & Bacon.

Kronowitz, E. L. 1992. *Your first year of teaching and beyond*, 2d ed. New York: Longman.

Manera, E., ed. 1996. *Substitute teaching: Planning for success*. West Lafayette, Ind.: Kappa Delta Pi, International Honor Society in Education.

Tauber, R. T. 1995. *Classroom management: Theory and practice*, 2d ed. New York: Harcourt Brace.

Warner, J., C. Bryan, and D. Warner. 1995. *The unauthorized teacher's survival guide*. Indianapolis: Park Avenue.

Wong, H. K., and R. T. Wong. 1991. *The first days of school: How to be an effective teacher*. Sunnyvale, Calif.: Harry K. Wong Publications.

Web Sites

www.yahoo.com/education/k_12
Yahoo, one of the major search engines for the World Wide Web, takes searchers to a wealth of K–12 educational materials and resources.

www.yahoo.com/recreation/travel/virtual_field_trips
Links to virtual field trips of K–12 interest. Many are interactive and include lesson plans.

www.yahoo.com/education/k_12/teaching/lesson_plans
Links to lesson plans in all content areas of K–12 interest.

www.col-ed.org/lessons_page.html
This site from the Columbia Education Center provides lesson plans organized by topic (science, math, language arts, social studies, miscellaneous) and grade levels K–12.

www.col-ed.org/smcnws/msres/curriculum.html
Offers Internet-based lesson plans and resources for teachers and students.

www.clarityconnect.com/webpages/terri/sites.html
Links to great sites for math teachers.

www.teachnet.com/how-to/manage

Provides classroom-management ideas, mostly for elementary and some for middle and high school.

www.teachnet.com

Offers a variety of tools for K–12 teachers, including projects, discussion groups, tips for classroom decor, organization and time management, lesson plans, classroom public relations, and humor.

www.ceismc.gatech.edu/busyt

The Busy Teachers' Web site provides teacher resources and ideas, projects by curriculum area for secondary teachers, a separate elementary section, and links to quality educational Web sites.

www.askeric.org/virtual/lessons

Lesson plans from ERIC.

www.ed.gov

Gives access to the U.S. Department of Education (ED) home page and links to current information in education and ED-funded Internet resources.

www.middleweb.com

Offers help for new middle school teachers. Provides articles and links about curriculum, teaching strategies, professional development, parent involvement, and assessment.

www.kdp.org

Offers a wealth of insights on topics of interest to the first-year teacher. Links and resources provide a rich array of writings, lesson plans, classroom suggestions, and commentary.

www.doubletakemagazine.org/edu/teachersguide

Offers thematic units of study on race relations, work, sense of place, political ideology, and sense of identity.

www.webteacher.org

Offers tutorials on Web technology.

Lesson 9 Summary

In this lesson, you took time to look forward in your teaching career and to consider your professional development. Next, you considered some concerns that are common to novice teachers who are transitioning to apprentice teachers and found some suggestions for handling those issues. Finally, you reviewed a list of some recommended print and online resources.

Notes & Ideas

Final Thoughts

Your first year of teaching is one of the most exciting times of your life. It is the reward for all the hard work you put into preparing yourself for this role. Now you have the opportunity to practice all that you have learned.

As you prepare your classroom, remember to establish and maintain a support system. Include your family, your new colleagues, friends, and peers with whom you established a network throughout your teacher-preparation program. These people can offer emotional support and lend a helping hand.

It is our hope that *Ready, Set, Teach! A Winning Design for Your First Year* will help you with the thousand-and-one questions new teachers face as they deal with the day-to-day realities of classroom life.

Be PROUD. You are a TEACHER!

References

Bloom, B. S., ed. 1984. *Taxonomy of educational objectives: Book 1: Cognitive domain.* New York: Longman.

Chaika, G. 2000. Help! Homework is wrecking my home life! *Education World.* Available at: *www.education-world.com/a_admin/admin182.shtml.*

Charles, C. M. 1992. *Building classroom discipline,* 4th ed. New York: Longman.

Edwards, C. H. 1997. *Classroom discipline and management,* 2d ed. Upper Saddle River, N.J.: Merrill.

Enz, B., and B. J. Carlile. 2000. *Coaching the student teacher: A developmental approach.* Dubuque, Iowa: Kendall-Hunt.

Fenstermacher, G. D., and J. F. Soltis. 1986. *Approaches to teaching.* New York: Teachers College Press.

O'Rourke-Ferrara, C. 1998. 'Did you complete all your homework tonight, dear?' Unpublished manuscript. ERIC ED 425 862.

Postman, N. 1995. *The end of education: Refining the value of school.* New York: Knopf.

Stamm, J., and C. Wactler. 1997. *Philosophy of education workbook: Writing a statement of beliefs and practices.* New York: McGraw-Hill.

Steffy, B., M. Wolfe, S. Pasch, and B. Enz, eds. 2000. *Life cycle of the career teacher.* Thousand Oaks, Calif.: Corwin.

Index

A

Academic achievement, 39
Achievement,
    academic, 39
    student, 53–55
Analysis, 54
Application, 54
Apprentice phase, 68, 70–71
Assessing-your-stress survey,
    61–62
Assessment,
    professional skills and
        attributes, 3, 7–9
    professional style, 3–5
    resources, 73
    rubrics, 53, 58–59
Assignment aide routine, 48
Attendance, 26–27
    records, 20
Attention signal routine, 47
Audiovisual equipment, 16

B

Balance, 60
Behavior, 44, 49–50
    management, 70
Belief orientations, 3
Bloom's Taxonomy, 53–54, 75
Books, 71
Breaks, 64

C

Cabinets, 16
Calendar, 20, 64
Career, 67
Checklists,
    instructional skills, 7–8
    professional attributes
        self-assessment, 8–9

Classicist teacher, 5
Classroom,
    community, 29
    floor plan, 13–14
    inventory, 15–16
    management, 43–51, 71–73, 75
    observation, 70
    setting up, 11–12, 15, 17
Collaboration, 13
Colleagues, 6, 12, 65
Communication, 12
    with parents, 35–42
Community,
    classroom, 29
    school, 12
Comprehension, 54
Conference planner, 39–40
Conferences,
    parent/teacher, 35, 39
    professional, 71
Consequences, 49
Contact logs, 21

D

Daily plan, 20
Deadlines, 20
Disabilities, 72
Discipline, 44, 49, 71, 75
Distinguished phase, 69
District, 6, 71

E

Effort, 54–55
Elementary teachers, 25, 27, 30–31
E-mail, 65
Emeritus phase, 69
Equipment, 15–16
Evaluation, 54
Executive teacher, 3, 5

Expectations, 53
Expert phase, 69

F

Filing cabinets, 16
First days of school, 24–34
Floor plan, 13–14
Folders for substitutes, 65–66
Four-square questionnaire, 27, 29
Furniture, 15–16

G

Getting to know you chart, 30
Grade books, 55–56
Grades, 53–55
Greeting students, 25–27

H

Homework, 36, 39, 41–42, 75
Humanist teacher, 5

I

Instructional,
    beliefs survey, 3–4
    skills, 70
    skills checklist, 7–8
Introduction letter, 36–37
Inventory, 12, 15–16

J

Journals, 71

K

Knowledge, 54

L

Learning contracts, 53, 57
Learning environment, 12–15
Lesson plans,

first day, 31–33
format, 22–23
notebook, 19–21
resources, 72–73
Life cycle of the career teacher,
    67–69, 75
Lifelong learning, 67
Long-term plan, 21

M

Mail, 65
Management,
    behavior, 70
    classroom, 43–51, 71–73
Materials, 15–16
Measurements,
    student learning, 52–59
    types, 53–54
Mentors, 70–71
Middle school,
    classroom, 14
    routines, 48
    students, 27
    teachers, 26–27, 30, 39
Model, reflection-renewal-growth
        cycle, 69

N

Nametags, 25–27
Newsletters, 38
Novice phase, 68, 70

O

Orientation to area, 13

P

Paper planning, 14–15
Parent/teacher conferences, 35, 39
Parents, 6

Phone messages, 65

Planning, 18–23, 64–65, 72

    lessons, 22–23, 31–33

    notebook, 19–21

Portfolios, 55–56

Preparation, 18

Primary,

    classroom, 14

    routines, 47

    teachers, 25, 27, 30–31, 39

Print materials, 71

Prioritizing, 65

Procedures, 45–48

Professional,

    attributes self-assessment

        checklist, 8–9

    development, 67–74

    phase, 68

    resources, 68, 71–73

    transitioning, 70–71

Professionalism, 2, 10

    roles and responsibilities, 3,

        5–7

    skills and attributes, 3, 7

    style, 3–5

Q

Question-and-response

    techniques, 44

Questionnaires,

    four-square, 27, 29

    study buddies, 31

Quick reference, 19

R

Reflection, 70

Reflection-renewal-growth cycle

    model, 69

Relationships, 25

    establishing, 27–31

Report cards, 55

Resources,

    lesson plans, 72–73

    professional, 68, 71

    quick, 19

Routines, 44–46

    before and after school, 64

    middle school, 48

    primary, 47

    secondary, 48

Rubrics, 53, 58–59

S

Scheduling, 31–33

School, 6

    community, 12

    district, 6, 71

Seating,

    charts, 26

    students, 25–27

Secondary,

    routines, 48

    students, 27

    teachers, 26, 30, 33, 39

Storage cabinets, 16

Stress, 60–64

Student(s), 6–7

    achievement, 53–55

    engaging, 44–45

    information letter, 27–28

    jobs, 64

    progress, 36, 39

    roster, 19

    teachers, 75

Study buddies questionnaire, 31

Substitute teachers, 60–61, 65–66,

    72

Supplies, 16

Support, 71

Surveys,

    instructional beliefs, 3–4

    assessing-your-stress, 61–62

Symbolic grading systems, 53–54

Synthesis, 54

T

Teach-a-bility, 15

Teachers, 31

    apprentice, 71

    elementary, 25, 27, 30–31

    middle school, 26–27, 30, 39

    primary, 25, 27, 30–31, 39

    secondary, 26, 30, 33, 39

    student, 75

    substitute, 60–61, 65, 72

Think-pair-share strategy, 45

Time management, 60–61, 65

    resources, 73

    strategies, 64

Traffic flow, 15

V

Variety, 45

Virtual field trips, 72

W

Web sites, 71–73

Week-at-a-glance, 23

Weekly,

    newsletter, 38

    plan, 20, 23

Work space, 13, 15

Workload, 60

Workshops, 70

New Teacher Advocate

It's a support system at your fingertips!

- **Practical**—classroom tips from those who've lived it,
- **Personal**—inspiring stories from and about teachers who care, and
- **Preeminent**—Ed Press award-winning newsletter!

Subscribe now and get four issues for only $10!

800-284-3167

To see a glimpse of this reader-friendly quarterly, click on the "publications" link at *www.kdp.org*.

KAPPA DELTA PI
International Honor Society in Education

Brings you excellence and leadership in education.

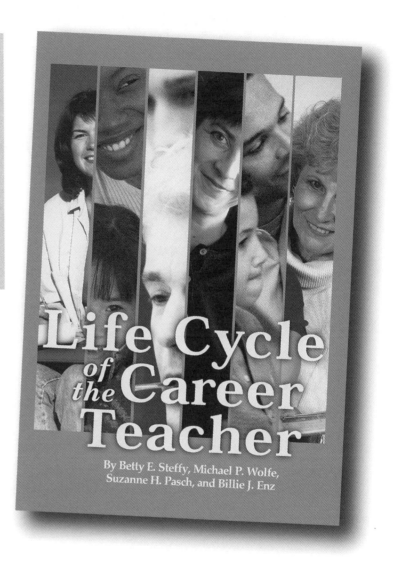

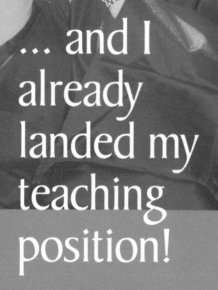

Ready, Set, TEACH!

Supporting teachers is a critical mission of Kappa Delta Pi, publisher of this book. The authors and editors hope that you've found this guide helpful and useful in preparing for your first year of teaching. We welcome your feedback—both compliments and criticism—so that we can continue to improve and provide educators with the best quality and most effective materials.

How would you rate this book?

Content ❑ Excellent   ❑ Good   ❑ Adequate   ❑ Poor

Format   ❑ Excellent   ❑ Good   ❑ Adequate   ❑ Poor

Would you recommend this book to others?

What section(s) did you find particularly helpful?

Please share your specific comments about the book.
Write them below or on the back of this page, if more space is needed.

If you would like to find out about other books and materials published by Kappa Delta Pi, visit our Web site at *www.kdp.org* or call (800)284-3167.

Please complete the personal information below so that we may contact you if necessary.

Name _____   Title _____

School/Affiliation _____

Street _____

City, State, Zip _____

Telephone _____   E-mail _____

Date _____

Photocopy or tear out this page and mail to: Marketing Director, Kappa Delta Pi, 3707 Woodview Trace, Indianapolis, Ind. 46268
Or FAX to: (317)704-2323
Or e-mail your comments to: webmaster@kdp.org